ROUTLEDGE LIBRARY EDITIONS:
WOMEN IN SOCIETY

I0124652

Volume 2

WOMAN AND SOCIETY

WOMAN AND SOCIETY

MEYRICK BOOTH

Routledge
Taylor & Francis Group
LONDON AND NEW YORK

First published in 1929 by George Allen & Unwin Ltd

This edition first published in 2025
by Routledge
4 Park Square, Milton Park, Abingdon, Oxon OX14 4RN

and by Routledge
605 Third Avenue, New York, NY 10158

Routledge is an imprint of the Taylor & Francis Group, an informa business

British Library Cataloguing in Publication Data
A catalogue record for this book is available from the British Library

ISBN: 978-1-032-87216-2 (Set)
ISBN: 978-1-032-86918-6 (Volume 2) (hbk)
ISBN: 978-1-032-87172-1 (Volume 2) (pbk)
ISBN: 978-1-003-53124-1 (Volume 2) (ebk)

DOI: 10.4324/9781003531241

Publisher's Note
The publisher has gone to great lengths to ensure the quality of this reprint but points out that some imperfections in the original copies may be apparent.

Disclaimer
The publisher has made every effort to trace copyright holders and would welcome correspondence from those they have been unable to trace.

This book is a re-issue originally published in 1929. The language used and views portrayed are a reflection of its era and no offence is meant by the Publishers to any reader by this re-publication.

WOMAN
AND
SOCIETY

Meyrick Booth
B.Sc., Ph.D.

London
GEORGE ALLEN AND
UNWIN LTD
Museum Street

FOREWORD

WE live in an age of rapidly changing values. This must be my excuse for adding another to the long list of books dealing with the Education, Life and Work of Woman.

Nearly all the more important works in this field (such as *Woman and Labour*) were published before the war. Since those days everything has changed. The immense development of Psychology, in particular, has opened up new social perspectives; and looking down these we find that the whole problem of Woman in relation to Society takes on a new form.

The present study is necessarily full of shortcomings. In the nature of things it cannot be more than a mere sketch, an attempt to suggest new lines of thought. But it may serve to carry the discussion a stage further. At the very least it should help to make it clear that the present chaos and insecurity in everything appertaining to Man and Woman and their social relations and functions is intolerable.

In certain quarters it may perhaps be suggested that it is not a man's business to write about Woman in general, or the Woman's Movement in particular. Is not the woman of to-day able to look after herself? But are there any women's problems that are not also men's problems? The interests of the two sexes are inextricably mingled.

The Education of Girls, the Work of Women in Industry, the Population Question, Sex Equality, Sex Psychology, Marriage, the Chaos in Sex Relationships, Genius and Sex

—are not all such subjects of equal concern to men and women alike?

All thoughtful people will agree that vital social problems cannot be dealt with in a fruitful way save through a whole-hearted co-operation between the two aspects of our common humanity.

MEYRICK BOOTH

LETCHWORTH, HERTS

CONTENTS

WOMAN AND SOCIETY

CHAPTER I

INTRODUCTORY—THE CRISIS OF TO-DAY

WE are still a long way removed from an adequate solution of the problem of Woman and Society. The mere fact that the various aspects of woman's life and work are so heatedly discussed on every side is the best proof that our ideals and values are in a state of flux.

The disintegration of the traditional conception of woman's position in society was undoubtedly necessary, for we cannot pour new wine into old bottles. But having broken the old bottles, into what sort of vessels is it proposed to decant the wine of emancipated womanhood? That is the question of questions. The revolt against outworn forms does not give us new ones. While it was natural and inevitable that the Woman's Movement should concentrate on the breaking down of barriers and the liberation of pent-up forces, it is every day becoming clearer that the magic word "emancipation" is not synonymous with a new social synthesis.

The Movement did a great work in raising the status of women and in providing them with an immense field of opportunity. For unmarried women, in particular, it opened up a new world. But, like other movements of protest, it has been nourished mainly by opposition. Its strength has lain, all along, in the negation of the old order; and it has not yet brought to light any well-thought-out positive social philosophy. Confronted with the task of construction, the Feminist Movement reveals itself as divided. For example, some sections favour special legislation for the protection of women workers; but others are furiously opposed to any recognition of sex difference. Again, the right wing of the Movement is orthodox in a moral sense, and defends monogamy; while the left wing is enthusiastically in favour of easy divorce, the "companionate marriage", and other experiments in sex reform.

    .   .   .   .   .

Reading modern literature dealing with women's problems, we at once perceive that it is almost wholly propagandist. The feminists are far more concerned to "down" their opponents than they are to throw any real light on woman's life and work; while the anti-feminists are for the most part reactionaries, scenting danger to their own privileges in the advance of woman. The lack of objectivity, of the true spirit of unbiased investigation, is perhaps the chief hindrance to the discovery of a fruitful synthesis.

It is not obvious that we are making any definite progress whatever towards solving a problem absolutely vital to our civilisation.

Is it not possible to find new paths by which we can carry the whole discussion a stage further? Let us ask ourselves: Have not recent developments in biology, psychology, eugenics, and sociology in general, thrown any fresh illumination upon the life and work of woman, since these branches of knowledge touch it at so many points? The entire mental background of our social life is now something quite other than it was when our theme first began to excite popular attention. The discussion is now largely entangled in outworn modes of thought and stale phrases. What is needed to-day, if we are to make any progress towards a genuine elucidation of what, for want of a better term, I may still call the Woman Question, is fresh air, a new outlook, a *re-orientation* in the light of our advancing knowledge. We need to review the whole field of battle from a standpoint outside existing movements and "isms".

a. The Flight from the Home

It will be universally admitted that the pursuit of freedom, the cult of independence, personal and economic, is the characteristic feature of modern girlhood and womanhood.

The functional view of education, the preparation of girls for their specifically feminine life-tasks (marriage and maternity), has sunk wholly into the background. One might almost say that it has vanished from sight. In its place we have a purely individualistic and non-racial life-outlook, the origins of which are to be seen clearly in John Stuart Mill's *The Subjection of Women* (with its underlying assumption of sex homogeneity).

The typical girl of to-day absorbs a freedom-loving and ego-centric philosophy of life from earliest childhood. Her books, her companions, her social *milieu*, her school, frequently the home itself—all conspire to impress upon her a view of life which leaves on one side the functional aspect of womanhood. The ideal of the modern girl is "to live her own life", to be independent, to make a career, to challenge men in the work of the world. That she is a woman and not a man is with her (at any rate in not a few cases) rather a matter of regret than a determining factor in her conscious approach to life (the subconscious, of course, knows better!).

For this state of things the school is no doubt largely responsible. Most girls' schools are staffed by teachers more or less impregnated with the ideas of the Woman's Movement of pre-war days, or even of the last century. Their typical outlook is that of the independent and often masculinised bachelor woman. Their notion of sex equality is an approximation on the part of girls to boyish methods of work and play.

It is hence no matter for surprise that we now breed, by thousands, a type of girl who is entirely lacking in the sense of womanly function. I met recently a young woman of twenty, the finished product of one of the largest and most famous girls' public schools in England, and asked her what plans she had for the future: "Oh, I want to be independent —to go in for a career", she replied. "Of course, I might marry; but if I did I should not have any children." This in cold-blooded seriousness. Were this a solitary case, it would, of course, have little significance; but I dare wager that nearly every reader of these lines will himself know of at least one identical case.

A large proportion of modern girls are trained almost wholly with a view to celibate careers. Their entire education is sexless and utilitarian. The victorious invasion of the field of woman's education by masculine ideals has deprived the modern girl of a *distinctively* feminine life-outlook.

These developments have not taken place without good cause. In Olive Schreiner's *Woman and Labour* (chapters i and ii) we have a masterly analysis of the manner in which woman has gradually seen her former fields of work slip from her. In primitive communities, women worked on the land, ground corn, made bread, kept sheep, spun flax and wool, reared large families, educated their own children, and managed the entire household. The woman of those days could not complain that her life was empty.

It is valuable to note that Olive Schreiner, with an insight much superior to that of most present-day feminists, saw clearly that (apart from the question of certain political and social disabilities) the work of women in those days was more solidly grounded in the realities of life, and was more congenial to their natural gifts, than is the work of women to-day. The trouble with the modern woman is that she has really nothing to do which corresponds with her inborn faculties. Most of the careers now open to her are of a nature unsuited to the psychology of the normal girl (a fact quite insufficiently realised by Olive Schreiner, who was no psychologist). On the other hand, domestic life has so lost its significance that it no longer satisfies the very praiseworthy desire of the modern girl to live a full life. This is a fact of fundamental importance for the whole problem of feminine education.

On page 50 of *Woman and Labour* we read: "The changes which we sum up under the compendious term modern civilisation have tended to rob woman, not merely in part, but almost wholly, of her ancient domain of productive and social labour. . . . Our spinning-wheels are all broken, in a thousand huge buildings steam-driven looms produce the clothing of half the world. . . . Our hoes and our grindstones passed from us long ago, when the ploughman and the miller took our places . . . to-day steam often shapes our bread and the loaves are set down at our very door; . . . the history of our household drinks we know no longer; we merely see them set before us at our tables. Day by day machine-prepared and factory-produced viands take a larger and larger place in the dietary of rich and poor, till the working-man's wife places before her household little that is of her own preparation, while among the wealthier classes, so far has domestic change gone that men are not unfrequently found labouring in our houses and kitchens, and even standing behind our chairs ready to do all but actually place the morsels of food between our feminine lips. . . . In modern cities our carpets are beaten, our windows cleaned, our floors polished, by machinery, or extra domestic, often male, labour. . . . Year by year, day by day, there is a silently working but determined tendency for the sphere of woman's domestic labours to contract itself. . . ." Olive Schreiner then goes on to show how the education of children, too, has more and more slipped away from home hands and become a specialised domain.

These sections of *Woman and Labour* present an illuminating picture of the fashion in which woman's life has become more and more empty of purpose, as her specific traditional spheres of interest have shrunk, with the dangerous result that woman tends (as in the days of the decadent Roman Empire) to become a parasite, a plaything of man, unless she joins the army of those who go in for some career of a more or less masculine (in the traditional sense of the term) type.

It is not necessary here to discuss the question whether or not this is gain. On the one hand, it is urged that life has lost heavily through the substitution of machine-made articles for the work of the loving hand, and that the girl working all day at a factory bench must sink to a lower mental level than her predecessor who had to attend to a hundred daily tasks, all demanding intelligence; on the other, that life has become easier and lighter, and that the entry of women into masculine fields enlarges the feminine outlook and enriches both sexes alike. At present, we merely note the fact that woman has not deserted the home sphere; *she has been driven out of it!* A final quotation from Olive Schreiner:

"Looking round . . . on the entire field of woman's ancient and traditional labours, we find that fully three-fourths of it have shrunk away for ever, and that the remaining fourth still tends to shrink."

The modern Anglo-Saxon girl finds herself growing up into a world in which there is little room for her to pursue those occupations which are traditionally associated with her sex, and for which she has in most cases more aptitude than for work in the modern man-made industrial world. She is thus thrust willy-nilly into the market-place. The schools have made haste to adapt themselves to the situation, and aim no longer at fitting girls for home-making.

It has thus come to pass that the ideal of the independent, self-supporting, ego-centric woman has won an almost complete triumph over the ideal of the woman who lives for the race and the home.

b. EMANCIPATION

If, as many people seem to think, the problem of woman's relation to society had been successfully solved through the flight from the home and the admission of women on equal terms to the different occupations and careers formerly followed by men, there would not be such a furious controversy about the whole matter.

The plain truth is that *the emancipation of women*, in the sense understood in the modern world, *has raised as many questions as it has answered.*

First comes the question : How long will woman herself be content with a type of emancipation which ignores the claims of all that is specifically feminine? The more recent publications of left-wing feminism show clearly enough that a certain section of thoughtful women are now in full revolt against the assumption that they have no personality of their own, but may quite properly be treated precisely as if they were men—although the very aim of the earlier type of feminism was to ensure that women should be treated like men !

More and more the racial point of view is making itself felt, so that one of the most widely read of modern feminists writes : "There never has been a period when education has trained women for the possibility of motherhood, and it is time that such training was begun." Nevertheless, another and larger wing of the Woman's Movement is still actively concerned to model the education of girls in every particular upon that of boys.

Which school of thought is going to win the battle?—the masculine-feminists who say: "Let women be as men in education and occupation"—the school which denies sex, and regards maternity, in the words of one of its exponents, as "a side-line"; or the feminine-feminists who see in woman the Mother and Race-bearer, and believe that the Woman's Movement is strongest when it most frankly takes its stand upon feminine function?

Another conflict rages around the question of "rights". If women are to share men's rights, the right to enter certain careers, the right to vote, to enter Parliament and so on, must they not, it is argued, also share men's responsibilities? Must not married women bear an equal share of the legal responsibility for the upkeep of the family; and should not the laws protecting women and giving them certain special sex privileges be repealed? This, in its turn, opens up the complex and difficult problem of the economic freedom of married women, upon which a whole literature has been written. The discussion of this topic, which began in the years just before the war, is still going on, and we are no nearer a satisfactory solution.

Here, again, we find fresh differences, not only between the feminists and the anti-feminists, but within the feminist camp itself. The hundred-per-cent. equalitarian feminists take up the logical position that women must have the courage of their convictions and be ready to drop all their legal and social privileges (see Chapter VI, *d* and *e*) to prove the sincerity of their plea for equality—even to the point of abolishing the husband's obligation to support his family. But another and much larger section adopts the view that women should grasp their new rights while not letting go of their privileges. These last point out, not without justice, that the protection of the family by the father is essential to maternity, and that without it the family would go to pieces. How many women, they ask, can take on the double task of bringing up children and earning an independent income under the stern conditions of modern life?

The different paths in the maze all return, sooner or later, to the same point: should sex be ignored, or is it a basic thing? Shall we accept the view of the out-and-out equalitarians, who declare that there is no difference between man and woman other than the purely physical (and regard this as of practically no importance); or are we to listen to the psychologists and biologists, who lay weight on the profound differences in mentality and instinct between men and women?

It will be found that this is, in reality, the key question. If we are clear upon this point, clarity will soon come to us in our examination of all the other questions. This book, accordingly, devotes a considerable amount of space to the subject of sex differences.[1]

. . . . .

The above represent a mere fraction of the social problems which remain unsolved, after the emancipation of women has become almost, if not quite, an accomplished fact. For the present they will be left on one side. My object in bringing them forward is merely to demonstrate that the

[1] Illustrative of the psychological tendency of modern sociology is the following passage from the concluding paragraph of Dr. McDougall's *Social Psychology*:

"the springs of all the complex activities that make up the life of societies must be sought in the instincts and in the other primary tendencies that are common to all men and are deeply rooted in the remote ancestry of the race";

and again in the Introduction to the same work:

"There are signs . . . that psychology will before long be accorded, in universal practice, the position at the base of the social sciences which the more clear-sighted have long seen that it ought to occupy."

Woman Question (which might almost as well be called the *Man* Question!) is still wholly unsettled. The existence of something very much like a dead-lock in respect of such problems as those indicated above will, however, in course of time, compel the discussion to enter upon a fresh phase.

It is transparently clear that not one of the more important issues involved can be settled by a further advance along the present road. Whether women do or do not penetrate into the few careers now closed to them is a matter that is hardly worth arguing about. This is not the real point of conflict. What difference would the opening of the Church, the Cabinet, the Admiralty, or the Foreign Office to women make to any one of the problems I have mentioned? None whatever. They are all of an ethical and psychological nature. There is not one of them that can really be settled unless we are prepared to get back to a definite view of woman's nature and social functions, to work out *a philosophy of woman* in relation to society.

The entire situation is in reality infinitely more complex than its statement in such works as *Woman and Labour* would lead us to suppose. It is there assumed that woman can throw off her sex (save for the purpose of child-bearing) and descend into the market-place, there to work side by side with man as an equal; and that in proportion as this takes place we shall establish a new commonwealth of equality of opportunity. These views are characteristic of the abstract and unreal life-outlook of the doctrinaire equalitarians. No one but an arm-chair intellectualist could suppose for a moment that woman will ever throw off her sex and dispense with the various privileges and advantages (imponderable and indefinable as many of these may be) which attach to it in the civilisation of the West.

The present situation is chaotic. It is unfair to women, because the equality held out is not one which really answers to their inner needs, and is therefore illusory. It is unfair to men, because at one moment they are compelled to yield a point to women under the plea of equality, and the next moment they must yield another under the plea of woman's sex privilege. (Consider, for example, the thousands of American wives who claim the right to travel about Europe with their husbands' money. What American husband would dream of seeing Europe with the money his wife earned while she stayed at home to work in a New York office?)

The root of the chaos lies in the utterly futile attempt to banish sex from the controversy.[1] Sex will not be banished. It lies at the root of all human society. The aim of the modern girls' school, to train the girl as co-worker with man, regardless of sex, leads to a host of anomalies and absurdities, with many of which we shall deal later. One of its first results is to fill the labour market with an army of pseudo-masculine young women, who have been divorced from woman's natural, organic relation to the home and the nurture of life (in the widest sense of the phrase) and flung in battalions into occupations which in no way correspond with their psychology. In this fashion thousands of men, the majority of whom would normally have married, and helped a corresponding number of girls to realise a more natural type of life, have been forced into unemployment; while countless young women are compelled to drag out an irksome existence as underpaid drudges in factory and office.[2]

In the usual approach to these grave problems from the side of the Woman's Movement there is little sign of any fruitful constructive principle. The feminists can hardly provide us with such a principle, because they are (for the

[1] As a feminist writer pathetically observes: "Humanity seems to find it so difficult to leave sex to itself."

[2] In the chapter entitled "The Vicious Circle" I deal with the quite erroneous idea that it is the numerical excess of women over men which compels so many women to seek independence.

most part) committed to a sexless view of society, and still
obstinately adhere to the individualism and utilitarianism
of Mill and his like. Their one idea—freedom, in the absence
of any synthetic principle, leads us no further. It has broken
down much that was rotten; but it cannot build up. In
practice, a purely negative philosophy of freedom merely
throws the young woman into the modern masculine type
of social system and leaves her to sink or swim. It makes no
attempt to remould our social life with definite reference to
feminine ideals and needs. No adequate solution of the
problem of woman and society can be put forward by those
who do not possess a definite positive conception of woman
as a being with a life and individuality of her own distinct
from that of man.

c. PHRASES AND REALITIES

The time has come to ask the question: Is the alternative
postulated by Olive Schreiner really inescapable? Is it true
that the path of modern woman divides according to the
signposts Masculinism and Parasitism?

We are told that the flight from the home is an accomplished fact which it is useless to resist, and that there is
really nothing to be done but to resign ourselves to an
inevitable process called "progress", which amounts in practice to nothing save the merging of the feminine part of
humanity in the vast machine of industry and "business".
There is even a large section of present-day opinion which
regards this masculinisation of women as desirable in itself,
passing with amazing superficiality over all the deep differences of mentality and instinct which distinguish the sexes.

The main purpose of the Woman's Movement is to enlarge
the life of woman and to give her richer opportunities of
development—opportunities in no way inferior to those

enjoyed by man. This book represents an effort in the same direction, but along another road.

The singular obliviousness of the human and psychological side of the problem, which has all along been so characteristic of the Movement, is natural enough in view of the superficial Victorian rationalism of the original leaders of the emancipation; but now that we possess a far deeper knowledge of mind and body than was then available, this type of thought has become impossibly naïve, and, in its practical results, pernicious.

It is of the first importance to examine very sharply the various catchwords which in the modern world take the place of thought. We all know those which are here especially in question: "equality", "independence", "self-development", "removal of sex barriers", and so on. What can equality mean, save that a woman should enjoy opportunities no less valuable than those enjoyed by a man? For *absolute* equality is not possible between beings with different functions. What becomes of the idea of equality when a man says, "I claim the right to enjoy the thrilling experience of motherhood"? It is clear that this equality of opportunity can only come about through a careful consideration of the essential differences of sex. A man cannot be equal to a woman in the field of maternity, but he can enjoy what will be, for him, experiences of equal value. And in a reverse sense, if women cannot be sailors or coal-miners, they may realise their potentialities in other ways more suitable to their physical structure. The attempt on the part of a few fanatical equalitarians to deny altogether the existence of any differences of significance between men and women is so purely doctrinaire, so unscientific and obscurantist, that it is not worthy of any serious consideration.

What is the inwardness of the ideal of independence held out before the girl of to-day? Is it not, in nine cases out of ten, the acceptance of a life-aim borrowed from the masculine side of life? And does not the much-coveted independence often end in an economic slavery as grinding as anything endured by the unemancipated woman of a hundred or more years ago? (In passing, I must remark upon the quaint delusion that a woman working from morn to night in a stuffy office for a man who is nothing to her is "free"; while a woman who works in her own home for herself, and a man chosen by herself, is a " slave" !)

Again, can we assign any clear meaning to the idea of self-development (the key idea of the Emancipation Movement) save in the sense that a woman should be free to express her own inner nature? If a girl who would like to be a happy mother finds herself spending her days in front of a machine, is this self-development? The fully developed self-conscious woman cannot realise her true self through the imitation of man. Woman is so deeply rooted in the world of personal relationships and racial instincts that she can never permanently thrive in the arid soil of a de-humanised and technical type of life. The case against "independence", in the sense of the cheap catchword, is that it means *dependence*—upon the man-made machine of commercialism.

Such are some of the points which force themselves upon us in reviewing the situation of to-day. In further sections of this work we shall return to them in detail.

For the moment let us take note of the barrenness of the ego - centric, pseudo - masculine life - ideal when confronted with the deep issues involved. The cult of individual freedom, alone, cannot solve the complex problems involved in the relationship of woman to society; for these take us at once into waters far deeper than those explored by the rationalists and utilitarians of the last century. This solution can be effected only by a courageous facing of all the realities of the situation in the light of modern knowledge; and especially it must depend upon the sympathetic co-operation of enlightened men and women.

.   .   .   .   .

It is now clear that the Woman's Movement has come to a crisis in its development. For long its chief *raison d'être* was to act as door-opener for women desirous of entering what had hitherto been regarded as masculine fields of work. This task is now virtually achieved. The doors have swung on their hinges, and most of them have been found to open into apartments in which the normal woman does not feel particularly comfortable. In any case, comfortable or otherwise, the girl of to-day can now enter any room she likes; and the Movement's janitorial functions being ended, it must either develop a new purpose or cease to be of significance. Feminism must either progress or perish. If it remains wrapped up in its philosophy of pseudo-masculinism, obstinately refusing to see in woman anything more than a replica of man, it cannot possibly exert any formative influence upon future events, for, by its own confession, it cannot give society anything more than could be given by an equal number of men. There is only one path of advance. The Movement must accept the vital significance of human bi-polarity for the whole of our social life as its basic principle.

Thus grounded in reality, the Woman's Movement of the future will seek to educate a generation of women rich as may be in all the essential characteristics of womanhood, and to create for them wide and fruitful fields of work, in which the opportunities of self-realisation will be no whit inferior to those which men have carved out for themselves. Thus will the feminine half of the race bring its full weight to bear in the common task of civilisation.

CHAPTER II

THE VICTORY OF MASCULINISM

IN Mr. Hutchinson's novel, *This Freedom*, we see how an energetic young English girl, born in very ordinary provincial surroundings, realises, as she comes more and more into contact with life, that it is men who count, men who have the "best time", men whose outlook imposes itself upon the world. She feels that she is "only a girl", that women are creatures of quite secondary importance. She forms the view that the only way to make her life worth living is to imitate men in every possible way, thus demonstrating her "equality". To this girl everything which is womanly, in the traditional sense of the term, seems narrow, unprofitable, second-rate, stultifying. We further see, as the tale proceeds, how she carries these views into her life, adopts a career, and marries on the understanding that she will be able to carry this on side by side with her home-life. Although not outwardly unhappy, the marriage ends in disaster and catastrophe; and the children realise, if the mother did not, how essential to life is the much despised femininity and its ideals.

If this novel dealt with people of a very exceptional type, it would be of no significance in the present connection. It is unfortunately only too true to the conditions of life and standards of value in present-day England. I am convinced that the majority of modern English girls do really think and feel like Mr. Hutchinson's heroine; and even if their subsequent lives do not end in palpable tragedy, the mischief that is done through their false values is widespread.

While not denying a historical necessity in the revolt of woman against the too narrow limitations of old-fashioned family life, we must admit that Mr. Hutchinson is right in his exposure of the disastrous error underlying the outlook of the modern feminist. The root evil lies in the failure of so many women to value highly enough the qualities and possibilities of their own sex. So far from the modern woman being, as is often stated, too independent, the exact reverse is the case—in a psychological sense. She has sunk into a state of unprecedented dependence upon men. Never before have masculine ideals triumphed so completely over the feminine side of life.

The explanation of the present-day state of affairs lies in the fact that we have no clear-cut philosophy of life giving us positive conceptions of the "manly" and "womanly". All is vagueness and uncertainty. We live in a chaos of individual opinions in which positive values have suffered dissolution. The modern woman is thus left suspended in mid-air. She has cast off the former ideals of womanhood, but has not yet reached the stage of formulating an inspiring new ideal.

Thus left without a life-ideal of her own, woman has surrendered to the superior positivity of man. The search for wider fields of work has come to mean, in practice, little more than the penetration of women into what were previously masculine fields. It must never be forgotten that the masculine careers into which the young woman of to-day so eagerly and so successfully forces her way were built up by men for men, without the slightest reference to the special needs of women. In adapting herself to these careers it is the woman who, with native plasticity, is adjusting herself to a masculine mould. It is not women who are conquering a new world, but men who are extending the area of their sphere of influence to include whole territories previously occupied by women.[1]

A generation or more ago the influence of the world of

---

[1] Cf. the early sections of *Woman and Labour*.

business and industry was confined mainly to the male sex. Now, the modern economic system (a machine wholly masculine in its form and influence) has expanded its sphere to include armies of women who possessed formerly a sphere of their own, which, if narrow, was, at any rate, *distinctive*. Every year thousands of girls are swallowed up alive in our factories, offices, and shops, and compelled to submit to a system of life which has about it absolutely nothing which in any way corresponds with their own distinctive qualities. The modern girl does not raise an army of her own, under her own flag. She merely enlists in the male army and serves under alien colours.

The girl of to-day has fallen almost completely under the spell of masculine ideals. She follows where men have gone before. In her ideals, her language, her education, her occupations, her outward appearance—nay, in her very thoughts, she has become masculinised to an extent that would have seemed to those living a few years ago not only unnatural, but purely incredible.

The revolt against her own sex is to be seen in the type of dress affected by the modern girl, in her close-cropped hair, in her walk, in her attitudes, in her slangy talk—a mere imitation of the talk of her boy friends; and in her desperate efforts (sometimes amounting to self-imposed starvation) to remove from her figure every suggestion of those womanly curves which differentiate her natural appearance from that of the male. As the last extravagance of this mode it is now reported in the Press that in Paris, New York, and other centres of advanced civilisation, establishments have been opened where women can have their breasts removed by surgical means, in order thereby to achieve the fashionable male figure!

All these things, although, in many cases, of apparently superficial importance, are nevertheless of great psychological

interest. At the very least, they indicate that the girl of
to-day has lost confidence in her own femininity, and with
a typically feminine lack of originality can, for the time being,
find nothing better to do than to mould herself on the
prevailing masculine lines.[1]

There appeared recently in the *Vossische Zeitung* (a leading
Berlin paper) a profoundly interesting article by Gina
Kaus, which emphasised the sense of inferiority which
modern civilisation creates in the mind of woman. A general
under-valuation of womanhood is (says the writer) implicit
in modern life, the orientation of which is wholly masculine.
The sex function of women, with all that it means of suffering
and responsibility, is felt by the typically modern girl as
a form of injustice, rather than (as should be the case) as
a high distinction. The brother is proud of being an airman
or a sailor; but the sister feels a sense of shame in being

[1] The following extract from a recent article in the *Manchester
Guardian*, by a leader of feminism, speaks volumes. The reference is to a
successful professional woman: "She is a modern woman in the best
possible sense of that much abused adjective—modern because she has
struck out a line for herself—has worked exactly as a man works; and
a woman may be forgiven for saying that she is modern, too, because
she has shown what women can and will do in the future." To do
exactly what a man does is to strike out a line for herself! What a revelation of the bankruptcy of all true originality in the modern woman.

The following adjectives are all taken from quite recent articles on
the girl of to-day in reviews and newspapers: sensible, level-headed,
sane, candid, frank, unsentimental, wholesome, clear-sighted, clear-eyed,
hard, independent, calculating, fresh, free, eager, vigorous, strenuous,
fearless, truthful, efficient, sturdy, sport-loving, direct, flippant, irresponsible, happy, cheerful, joyful, healthy, clean, honest, kindly.

These constitute an almost complete list of the terms employed.
Most striking is the total absence of all adjectives suggesting traditionally
feminine qualities, e.g. sympathy, grace, tenderness, intuition, gentleness, or devotion. That the girl of to-day has actually lost these attributes
is not to be believed, but it is extremely suggestive that in none of
these articles, nearly all of which were in praise of her, is the slightest
weight laid upon any qualities that might not just as well be exhibited
by any boy.

a woman. She feels she is the victim of a great injustice on
the part of nature. She wants to be a boy. "Manhood
appears to her as synonymous with superiority"; and early
in life she forms an "inferiority complex". This complex
causes her to strive with all her might towards all that is
masculine. "It is this struggle to be manly that imparts to
the present-day girl her surprising energy and almost
violent activity." The modern girl tends to see men at once
as objects of admiration and imitation, and as the enemies
of her sex (since in the girl's eyes man, as the sex partner,
appears responsible for maternity—now regarded rather as
a curse than a privilege).[1]

In Germany, too, one of the most valued of modern
thinkers, Georg Simmel, has strongly emphasised the one-
sided masculinism of present-day life: state, laws, morals,
religion, science—all are almost exclusively male in their
origin and present form. In consequence, we do not value
objectively. Our whole outlook is too masculine; and some
of the most important aspects of civilisation (those more
especially related to the characteristically female realm of

[1] Cf. also *Hypatia*, by Mrs. Bertrand Russell, p. 21, where, speaking
of modern girls' education of the average kind, she says:
"Is there something wrong with this education of women, and, if so,
what? I think we must judge that there is. The reason lies in the sense
of inferiority bred in women by so much oppression, and the natural
result that their chief aim, as they struggled upwards, was to prove
that in all respects they were just as good as men. The second aim was
to prove that they could jolly well do without them. In exactly the
same way the worker, rising in the social scale, seeks to prove himself
a bourgeois. Both efforts are mistaken. Each class and sex has that to
give to the common stock of achievement, knowledge, thought, which
it alone can give, and robs itself and the community by inferior
imitation. . . . Many an ardent feminist spinster in a girls' secondary
school has sighed over the state of public opinion which forced her to
drive her girls' minds along channels for which they were not always
suited, that they might do well at college and show that women could
surpass the men. . . . Feminist ideals of education, then, had the defect
that they did in a certain measure deny sex or ignore it."

human, personal, and domestic life) are neglected. The discontent of the modern woman is adequately explained by the fact that in this *milieu* she very naturally feels like a fish out of water.

.   .   .   .   .

The lack of a positive feminine ideal makes itself felt throughout the whole educational system, but more especially in the larger girls' High Schools and in the Universities.

During the spring of 1927 one of the large London dailies ran a correspondence on the Education of Girls. One of the most striking letters was from a lady who wrote:

"I am an Oxford resident, all my life a strong feminist, and yet I think the education of women in this University a deplorable mistake. Women in Oxford are merely poor imitations of the men. Their colleges, clubs, games, recreations, even their dress, are modelled on those of the men. Glorious young womanhood is content merely to ape in feeble fashion the sex it should inspire."

The leaders of female education in this country have strangely enough failed to perceive that the doctrine of sex equality, when accompanied by *a complete refusal to recognise the positive worth of what is distinctively feminine*, must result (at any rate logically) in the total elimination of the idea of womanhood from our social and educational system, since all standards and values must now be derived from the masculine world.

It will be said that all these matters are of no importance; that girls are sure to retain their natural womanhood, no matter how they are educated; that the power of heredity is so great that no efforts of ours can alter the reality of sex; and that there is therefore no cause for anxiety lest our girls should lose anything of their essential femininity. The reply to all such arguments is easy. If our efforts to work against nature are really so futile, then why make them at all? Why pursue these paths if it is so sure that they do not lead anywhere? Many feminists are amusingly illogical in this respect. At one time they tell us that it is of the utmost importance that we should do all we can to bridge the gulf between the sexes and to establish sex equality, that women should demonstrate the fact that they are, after all, not inherently different from men, and can properly pursue every sort of masculine occupation. At another, in response to some murmur that women might lose much of their value by sinking their individuality in that of the opposite sex, they hasten to inform us that we need entertain no such fears, because the gulf created between man and woman is so profound that it can never be bridged. Even Olive Schreiner, who avoided some of the more glaring fallacies of the early school of feminism, is here guilty of an almost incredible self-contradiction. In *Woman and Labour* (in the sections "Woman and War" and "Sex Differences") she is much concerned to convince us that sex is very much less important than is usually assumed; and that practically all supposedly masculine pursuits can well be carried out by women; in fact, that what we call sex is largely a product of false environment and education. But in the section entitled "Some Objections" she finds it necessary to come to grips with the loss of individuality argument, and we learn to our surprise that the significance of sex is so profound, and it penetrates so deeply into the heart of reality, that we need have no sort of fear that the entry of women into the professions, etc., should in any way render them unfeminine or less capable of inspiring emotion in the opposite sex. We are even told that sex "plays still to-day on earth the vast part it played when hoary monsters ploughed after each other through Silurian slime ". The average reader will draw from this latter line of thought, not the conclusion aimed at by the writer (namely, that sex, being ineradicable, may safely be ignored in education and occupation), but the much more obvious deduction that a factor so ancient and so deep-seated cannot possibly be left out of account in the organisation of our educational and social life!

This is but one of the many contradictions which have developed in the Woman's Movement through its lack of a definite philosophy of sex. The sincerity and idealism of so many feminists cannot in the long run hide the fact that the logical foundations of the Movement are unsound. The attempt to pass over the entire problem of sex distinction must lead in the end to numerous absurdities, of which the above is only a single example. If we start with the assumption that women are not essentially different from men in their mental and instinctive life, we are bound to stumble from one impossible position into another, because the basis of our reasoning is false. The contradiction between the sexless equalitarianism of the feminists, on the one hand, and their continual insistence, on the other hand, that women should be represented on all sorts of public bodies in order that the "woman's view-point" should be voiced, is one that runs right through the Movement. It is never realised, apparently, that the denial of a vital psychological distinction between man and woman entirely does away with the force of the plea for woman's view-point. Why must the woman's voice be heard? Obviously because she has something to say which emanates from another type of mentality. The whole force of the Feminist Movement must, logically speaking, be enhanced in proportion as we emphasise and define the characteristic nature of woman and the special value of her contribution to public matters.

.   .   .   .   .

A most interesting light on the spirit of present-day English feminism is thrown by the articles which recently appeared in *Time and Tide* written by the distinguished lady who uses the name "Candida". Here we see with great clearness (more often between the lines than in what is directly urged) to what an extent the mind of the modern woman has been conquered by masculine ideals. A special word of praise is bestowed upon the founders of the large girls' schools for their endeavour to produce a generation of "independent, free-spirited, courageous, responsible citizens". As a reaction against narrow domesticity this aim was praiseworthy; and I do not wish to appear ungrateful to such women as Miss Beale, Dame Lumsden, Miss Davies, or Miss Dove for much excellent work they gave to the country. But is it not clear that the above ideal has absolutely nothing *distinctively feminine* about it?[1] And what is meant by "responsible"? From the standpoint of the functional conception of society, a woman's responsibilities are essentially other than those of a man, because her functions are different. It is precisely against this sexless view of education that my protest is levelled. It is utterly unpsychological. Not a word is here of woman's unique qualities and *their* education! Intuition, affection, sensibility, personal devotion,

---

[1] As the feminists are fond of referring to George Eliot with pride as a specimen of female intellect, perhaps they will listen to what she had to say upon this very matter. In August 1868 she wrote to Miss Emily Davies, the foundress of Girton, urging her not to forget, in her efforts to further the education of girls, that they were fundamentally different from boys, and that the difference of sex is an important part of the spiritual wealth of humanity: "We can no more afford to part with that exquisite type of gentleness, tenderness, possible maternity suffusing a woman's being with affectionateness, which makes what we mean by the feminine character, than we can afford to part with the human love, the mutual subjection of soul between a man and a woman —which is also a growth and revelation beginning before all history." (From *Emily Davies and Girton College*, by Barbara Stephen, p. 181.)

maternal feeling, realistic sense, practicality, adaptability, tact—these are feminine characteristics in a sense quite other than freedom of spirit or independence. Could we have a better example of the fact that while in our boys' schools we really train boys along the lines of their inherent qualities, in the girls' schools there are no independent ideals? The entire tendency of thought above indicated reveals a total deficiency in positive ideals. Worst of all, this tendency is by no means confined to the schools more particularly in mind. For "Candida" goes on to remark that it extended speedily "to every girls' school in the country".[1]

It is one of the peculiarities of educational ideals that they tend to be at least twenty or thirty years behind the times, owing to the fact that the older teachers and head teachers have for the most part acquired their life-outlook at the schools and colleges they attended when they were young. A head mistress of fifty probably formed her ideas when she was between twenty and twenty-five. It is thus not difficult to see how it is that our present-day system of education has been so very little affected by all the immensely important advances of the last twenty years in psychology and sociology.

[1] That there is still a complete lack of feminine ideals in the big girls' schools is indicated by the following quotation from the *Morning Post* of July 5, 1928 ("Is the Public School Girl Becoming a Type?" by Phyllis Mégroz):

"THE TYPE THAT WILL EMERGE

"The long-established public schools for boys have yielded us a classifiable and traditionally superlative type; the existing, very much younger sister institutions have also produced a type of girl distinct from those not similarly trained. She is honest, courageous, sporting, perhaps a little inclined to be hard, but absolutely dependable, full of initiative and self-reliance.

"The opening of more and more public girls' schools spells the rapid evolution and spread of this type, and it is little to be doubted that the public school girl of the not distant future will represent, as does her brother, the public school boy, all that is best and most enduring in our fundamental education."

The vast majority of girls' schools, more particularly the large High Schools, are still floating in the backwash of Victorian rationalism and utilitarianism.

To remove a possible misunderstanding, I hasten to add that such ideals as those set up by "Candida"—freedom, independence, responsibility, and so forth—are not in themselves unworthy of the emphasis laid upon them by eminent pioneers of women's education. It is all a question of degree. It is no doubt beneficial to girls that they should, in addition to their own natural abilities, acquire a certain balancing modicum of more masculine attributes. It would be an excellent thing if the boys in a public school received a certain training in more feminine qualities, if they learned more sympathy, more gentleness, more patience and docility. But it would not be well if the process were to go too far! Nay, more, it would be good for boys to learn something of nursing, cooking, sewing, and the care of children. But granted all this, would not the whole world see something grotesque in a boys' school which aimed *in the first place* at inculcating such qualities as sympathy, or docility, or at giving a training in sewing or nursing? We all know that a boys' school must aim primarily at training along masculine lines. It must lay weight on independence, initiative, freedom of spirit, fair play, chivalry, and in general on all that is distinctive of our best manly traditions. Admirable as affection, emotion, gentleness, or adaptability may be in themselves, everyone will admit that boys whose training had tended to develop these qualities to the neglect of those more typically and naturally boyish would grow up into a generation of hopeless milksops. Such a system of masculine education would be ruinous to the national welfare. My charge against the girls' schools is therefore not that they lay stress on such ideals as freedom or independence, but that they do so to the exclusion of the more naturally feminine side of life. The mischief is that our modern girls' schools appear to be *founded upon masculine ideals*. Their philosophy of education is, in fact, as perverted as would be that of a boys' school which aimed chiefly at training its pupils in gentleness and sewing. Although, owing to the almost incredible loss of a proper sense of values which is a characteristic of our sophisticated society, people in general do not see anything amiss in girls being brought up along masculine lines, in reality the effects are as disastrous as they would be if boys were trained like girls.

Here we see what dire confusion results when an educational system has no definite philosophy of life behind it, when there are no clear-cut aims and logical distinctions. When once we have blurred our values to the point of no longer possessing any well-defined philosophy of sex distinction, we have departed from every sound principle that can guide our educational practice.

The doctrines of individualism, which, as we have seen, are still so influential in female educational circles, cause each particular girl to be looked upon as a separate unit, an autonomous being, not in any way organically related to the community or to the opposite sex. Upon this basis it is a foregone conclusion that we shall produce no adequate educational aims. The leaders of the female educational world have wholly lost sight of the immovable truth that men and women are *complementary opposites*. Each best fulfils itself by developing just those qualities lacking in the other. The full-developed polarity of sex is an indispensable dynamic in the evolution of civilisation.

In analysing the causes that have led to the masculinisation of modern girls' schools, we must assign due weight both to the ideal factors and the practical. On the one hand we have a complete absence of positive feminine ideals; on the other a series of powerful influences all tending to thrust the young woman of to-day into the professional and business world. The ideal and the practical act and react upon one another. It is very largely the decay of positive feminism that has led to the gross undervaluation and under-remuneration of all the more specifically womanly fields of work. House-work, the care of children, nursing, to take examples, are both undervalued and underpaid. Unless we assume, as indeed the modern world does assume, that machines are more important than human beings, we may well ask: Why should a skilled nurse, who undertakes the supremely important task of caring for ill human beings, be paid much less than the motor mechanic who overhauls our motor cars when they are out of order? In most families the children's maid, who looks after the heir of the house, is paid less than the head groom who looks after the horses! It is against this materialistic system of values that feminism should fight. It is my criticism of such feminists as Olive Schreiner that they urge women to leave their natural sphere of work and compete with men, instead of seeking to raise the entire level of women's work and pay so as to bring it up to the standards of masculine work. A nurse should be at least as highly trained and well paid as a motor mechanic. This line, the upward valuation of the specifically feminine, is the true line of advance.

CHAPTER III

PSYCHOLOGICAL

a. OUR FALSE IDEALS

IF a man be ill, the first condition of his recovery is that he should know that he is ill. Only then will he call in a doctor and undertake remedial treatment. The majority of those who are actively engaged in our educational system do not even admit that there is anything vitally wrong with it. It seems to them quite normal that hundreds of thousands of splendid young women of the better classes should consign themselves to celibate careers, and that the nation should depend for its future citizens on the swarming child-life of the slums. In reading present-day English educational periodicals one is again and again struck by the fact (which would seem almost incredible to, say, an Italian) that the young girl is not regarded in the least as a potential mother or race-bearer. The outlook is sexless and non-racial. It is assumed in a light-hearted way that the race will go on somehow, even if none of our girls marry. The entire point of view is so completely ego-centric, that one can easily see that the writers have never, even for an instant, supposed that there could be any other approach.

The first condition of progress is therefore a frank recognition of the falsity of our present ideals, and a full realisation of the sickness of the present system. The illness is not past healing if it be rightly diagnosed. There is in England an immense reservoir of first-class human material with which it would be possible to build up a magnificent civilisation by following the laws of biology and psychology. But we must liberate ourselves from the reckless individualism and utterly unbiological life-outlook of to-day.

This liberation may well begin, in the educational world,

by a new and much more psychological envisagement of the object of education—the adolescent girl. Getting rid of doctrinaire theories about sex equality, which cause those who hold them to become wilfully blind to the most obvious and important distinctions between boys and girls, let us simply ask the question: What is the nature of the growing girl, and under what conditions can she best develop?

We are continually brought back to a single central point—the lack in modern England of *a typical feminine life-ideal* capable of serving as a basis for the education of girls. Such an ideal alone can save girls' schools from degenerating into the rather thin imitations of boys' schools which they have now, for the most part, become.

No better motto could be found for the education of girls than one which I take from the pages of John Stuart Mill (when writing his *Subjection of Women*, Mill unfortunately forgot many of the principles which he had expounded in his own previous writings!):

"Human nature is not a machine to be built after a model, and set to do exactly the work prescribed for it, but a tree which requires to grow and develop itself on all sides, according to the tendency of the inward forces which make it a living thing." (*On Liberty*, chap. iii.)

It is precisely my charge against the present-day educational system that it *does* build girls "after a model"—a masculine model, while paying little attention to the "tendency of the inward forces". If anyone would maintain that the "inward forces" working in the mind and soul of the adolescent girl are not essentially different from those working in the opposite sex, I can only say that he must be totally ignorant of whole chapters in the story of modern psychology, and those amongst the most important which have been written. It may be true that in superficial matters, such as proficiency in arithmetic, languages, or science, the differences between the sexes are not of striking significance (although even here there are differences of some importance: see p. 186). It is necessary to look much deeper. It is just in the "inward forces" which make her "a living thing" that the girl profoundly differs from the boy. It is more especially in the inherent tendency of her subconscious, instinctive, and emotional life that the typical girl shows her femininity.

It is not those who, like myself, advocate a wise differentiation between the sexes who are the opponents of the progress and development of girls; but those who work against "the tendency of the inward forces" of the growing girl, by attempting to impose upon her a method of education and recreation which was originally designed for boys, and is in no way suited to the specific needs of girls. Violence is thus done to the nature of the growing girl, and for this she may have to pay a heavy price, either in damaged health or in a warped psychology.

On every hand we hear complaints from parents and others of the restlessness, discontent, and cynicism of the present-day girl. But the question is not often put: How much of this may be laid directly at the door of a system of education which fails to develop some of the most deeply seated elements of the girl's character (those which are more specifically feminine), because it prefers to concentrate on the training of those sides of her nature which she happens to have in common with boys? The modern boy receives an education which really rests upon a sound study of boyish psychology, and under this system he develops (speaking broadly) without severe inner conflicts or difficulties. But with the girl all is different. Her deeper psychology is so radically other than that of the boy, that it is only by doing considerable violence to a large portion of her personality that she is able to make a success of her school-life.

The great boys' schools, despite all their defects, are the

depositories of a long tradition, an immense experience of boyish ways and needs. The modern girls' school, on the other hand, is a new-fangled creation, evolved, for the most part, under the influence of an unpsychological pseudo-masculinism.

When the young woman of to-day has made her way through a type of school-life ill-adapted to her true needs, she goes out into the world of man-made values which now surrounds her, and is confronted with another hard problem, that of adaptation to a mode of life having almost no points of contact with her natural self.

And yet there are people who wonder why the modern woman is so discontented! And there are others who put her discontent down to the fact that she does not enjoy the same opportunities in all respects as a man—who think that when the few remaining "barriers of sex" have been broken down, all will be well; that all that women want is to be engineers, ministers of religion, sailors, or air pilots! What a strange delusion. What woman wants is what every living creature wants—namely, the chance to realise her potentialities, the opportunity to give employment to all the wonderful faculties with which she has been so richly endowed by Nature. The feminist offers her stones for bread.

Man is Apollonian. He is interested in form, in abstract thought. Woman is Dionysian. She is rooted in nature, in the elemental and life-giving. Watch any little girl delighting in flowers, kittens, or young puppies, in babies or dolls. Here she is in her element, in contact with young life. With a whoop of delight she rushes towards the kitten: "Oh, how perfectly sweet!" she cries. The while her brother sits on the floor, taking a toy watch to pieces, or runs down the street to where he can see the trains go by. When the boy grows up he is permitted to continue his interest in trains and machinery. Otherwise with the poor girl. She is not allowed to develop her interest in life. She is forcibly crammed with arithmetic, Latin, chemistry, or what not—subjects originally selected for boys, and although, of course, necessary in a girls' school, not suitable to serve as a basis for the curriculum.[1]

Further, the entire modern examination system, not the best for many boys, is poisonous when applied wholesale to girls' schools. The mere accumulation of abstract and often imperfectly assimilated knowledge, as necessitated by examinations, is in no way suited to the typical girlish psychology. It gives an unfair advantage to those girls who happen to possess an unusually masculine type of mind, and is another cause of the sense of inferiority which to-day obsesses the feminine girl, compelled to measure herself and to be measured by wrong standards. The examination of girls, if it is to reveal their potential usefulness to the community, should take into account innumerable qualities which cannot be expressed with pen and ink, but which are

[1] In *The English Miss*, by Mr. Mottram, a novel which is admittedly one of the most penetrating studies of English girlhood in our literature, we make the acquaintance of Marny, a child of the "super-healthy, emotion-fearing" upper-middle class of southern England, a girl who has a profound horror of all that is traditionally feminine: "She had read secretly and with blushes of how the [Amazonian] virgins mutilated their bodies in order to bend the bow. She would have done the same, had it not involved saying out loud what she would never say—that she was a woman. She did not deny her sex. She wanted to ignore it." Of particular interest is the conflict in Marny's development between her conscious self (which is moulded wholly along masculine lines) and her indestructible subconscious femininity. The latter—which is the girl's truest self—never attains to any full or harmonious development. Her whole life and education (which is admirably described) conspire to suppress and stifle her real inner nature. Whether this was the author's intention or not, readers of his novel are left with the impression that the deplorable moral collapse of Marny's intended husband was not unconnected with her own shortcomings as a woman.

vital to life and culture. For example: sympathy, intuition, capacity for dealing with children and invalids, reactions towards parents, tact in social matters, skill in managing a household—qualities associated with the girl's *racial* value, rather than with her capacity to compete with men in the market-place. It is, of course, true that in the case of a boy, too, many qualities may be of use to him in later life which will not serve him in the examination-room; but this truth is of much greater significance for the girl, since the real centre of gravity of her personality lies wholly outside the sphere which can be reached by the examiner's methods.

b. The School and the Mother

Leading psychologists, amongst others Havelock Ellis, the world-famous authority on sex psychology, and the late Dr. Stanley Hall, author of the standard work *Adolescence*, have repeatedly warned the educational world as to the dangers which must result from the totally unpsychological attitude of the modern school towards the adolescent girl.

In *Sex in Relation to Society* (chap. ii) Ellis writes: "It must always be remembered that in realising the especial demands of woman's nature, we do not commit ourselves to the belief that higher education is unfitted for a woman. That question may now be regarded as settled. There is therefore no longer any need for the feverish anxiety of the early leaders of feminine education to prove that girls can be educated exactly as if they were boys, and yield at least as good educational results. . . . It is now more necessary to show that women have special needs, just as men have special needs, and that it is as bad for women to force them to accept the special laws and limitations of men, as it would be for men to force them to accept the special laws and limitations of women."

On page 76 of the same work we find Ellis in agreement with Dr. Engelmann (the late distinguished American obstetrician), Dr. Kenealy,[1] and others, in the belief that violent muscular exercise and heavy muscular development in general is not beneficial to growing girls, and may have results that are really serious for their future efficiency as mothers. All those who wish to make a deeper study of the proper education of girls should not fail to read these chapters of *Sex in Relation to Society*—they contain invaluable material. They reveal a lack of consideration for the racial aspect of education on the part of the usual girls' school which is positively tragic.

As Ellis writes: "Women are more delicately poised (than men), and any kind of stress or strain, cerebral, nervous, or muscular, is more likely to produce serious disturbance, and requires an accurate adjustment to their special needs."

Completely ignoring all such expert opinion as the foregoing, a host of teachers all up and down the country are busily engaged in imposing man-made ideals of work and sport upon our all-too-impressionable young womanhood. During the most critical periods of development, when a girl needs to husband all her nervous energy in order that her ripening system should attain to full power, it is only too often the case that she is forced through a remorseless treadmill of routine, having no relation to her true needs.

From about the eleventh year till the seventeenth girls develop with great rapidity. Later on the growth is much slower. A girl of seventeen is years older than a boy of the same age. She is not far from full development, whereas the boy still has a long way to go before he reaches maturity.

[1] See *Feminism and Sex Extinction*.

Speaking generally (and of the northern races), a young woman of nineteen is at least as mature as a young man of twenty-four. This striking dissimilarity in growth-periods between the sexes is of fundamental importance for the educator. The greatest care should be taken in dealing with girls between the ages of eleven and seventeen. To put them through a curriculum similar to that demanded of boys is egregious folly.[1]

Dr. Arabella Kenealy writes (in *Feminism and Sex Extinction*): "The natural languors and disabilities of the girl's adolescent phase are vigorously combated. . . . The unfortunate young developing creature is exhorted, spurred . . . compelled by rigid rule, indeed, to take her part in strenuous exertions—with the aim of developing masculine muscles where feminine muscles should be. At the same time, her brain is forced, crammed, and exploited by perpetual mental tasks, by competitive examinations, or by some other strain of specialism, intellectual or industrial." In consequence we often get "Amazons of the hockey field, only just distinguishable in general characteristics from the male, and lacking more or less wholly in womanly psychology and aptitudes."

It is commonly supposed that the new régime has given us a type of girl much superior in health and capacity to the "fainting miss" of early Victorian or Georgian days. This is a complete delusion. The women of those times were undoubtedly less masculine than the girl of to-day, and less fitted for sport; but they were wonderfully vital and capable in their own particular sphere. After all, we must not forget that, as mothers, they produced such personalities as Dickens, Thackeray, Browning, Wordsworth, Gladstone, Stanley, Gordon, Darwin, Spencer, George Eliot, the Brontës, Jane

[1] The reader is referred to *Adolescence*, by Dr. Stanley Hall; also to *Das Seelenleben des Jugendlichen*, by Dr. Charlotte Bühler, of Vienna.

Austen, Florence Nightingale, Mrs. Fawcett, Mrs. Despard, Mrs. Butler, George Meredith, Rossetti, Swinburne, Shelley, Keats, Morris, and Thomas Hardy—to pick out a few names at random. We are constantly being informed that the independence of women will have the result of raising the standard of motherhood and giving us a higher type of child; but it will perhaps be just as well to reserve our opinion upon this matter until we have actually seen a generation which could fairly be placed side by side with the great men and women enumerated above. In the meanwhile we may well retain the conviction that the Victorian mother was a person of noteworthy efficiency and power.

Dr. Arabella Kenealy quotes Dr. Gaillard Thomas, the American gynæcologist, to the effect that "only about 4 per cent. of American women proper were physiologically fitted to become wives and mothers"; and Dr. Stanley Hall gives a large body of statistics (see *Adolescence*) showing the alarming unfitness of the Anglo-Saxon woman for maternity. Dr. Engelmann wrote: "It appears to be a fact that women who develop their muscular system highly suffer exceptionally in childbirth." Parenthetically, it may be remarked how very seldom we hear of successful maternal achievements on the part of any of the strenuous young women hockey, golf, or tennis players or swimmers whose pictures adorn our daily papers. A Vienna paper not long ago brought out some figures showing that the birth-rate amongst women prominent in athletic life in Austria was less than one-fifth of the rate amongst others of the same class who were not notably athletic—and even the latter rate was less than the death-rate in their class. Let those who believe the athletic activities of our young women are going to give us a higher race ponder these facts carefully. In this connection it is also noteworthy that while the general death-rate has been much improved, the deaths in maternity show no corresponding decline.[1] It is clear that there must be some strong cause holding back the improvement that we should have expected to see in this field, and it would seem by no means unlikely that a type of education which ignores the potential motherhood of the girl may play a large part in the matter.[2]

Many readers, while perhaps accepting the statement that the education of to-day does not do anything to prepare the girl for healthy motherhood, will say: "Well, at any rate we have got a generation of wholesome-minded, robust young women, quite different from the 'genteel accomplishments and smelling-salts' type of a generation or more ago!"

It is doubtful how far this confident belief will survive an examination of facts. A very large proportion of more or less serious breakdowns in health occur amongst girls going

[1] Deaths from childbirth per 1,000 births:

1911	..	..	..	3·87	1922	..	..	..	3·81
1912	..	..	..	3·98	1923	..	..	..	3·81
1913	..	..	..	3·96	1924	..	..	..	3·90
1914	..	..	..	4·17	1925	..	..	..	4·08
1920	..	..	..	4·33	1926	..	..	..	4·12
1921	..	..	..	3·91					

During this period of 15 years the *general* death-rate has declined from *ca.* 15 per 1,000 to 11·5 per 1,000.

[2] In *Population and Birth-Control*, edited by E. and C. Paul (section by R. Manschke), is a mass of statistics tending to show the ever-increasing unfitness for maternity of the woman of Western civilisation; the proportion of infant deaths due to congenital defects has more than trebled in a space of some fifty years in England and Wales (in 1860, 1·67 per 1,000 births; in 1900, 4·2; in 1905, 6·2), and the proportion of infants perishing of debility has more than doubled in the same period (1860, 12·7 per 1,000; 1905, 26·5 per 1,000). These figures (in both categories) are far more favourable amongst primitive populations—for example, in the latter category, in Galicia, the proportion is only from 1 to 2 per 1,000. Manschke draws special attention to the abnormally high maternal mortality in the New England States and in Australia.

In *The Nature of Woman*, Dr. Lionel Tayler writes that so far as can be judged, "at no time in history has childbirth been so difficult, so unhealthily difficult, as now, and . . . this has manifested itself chiefly in the last fifty years".

through the modern routine of school-life and professional training—a fact which will not be in the least surprising to anyone who has followed the argument of this chapter. In almost all institutions where men and women work side by side the cases of ill-health amongst the women are far more frequent than amongst the men.

In all probability we are here dealing with a misconception rooted in a superficial view of sex distinctions. It does not at all follow that because a girl plays hockey well, or, in general, that because she develops a heavy muscular system (not natural in a civilised woman), she will for this reason be really healthy. Some of the worst cases of hysteria and other serious nervous disorders occur amongst physically powerful, sport-loving girls. Health is not a question of physique alone. It depends largely upon a fine harmony between mind and body, and upon an accurate adaptation of means to ends. The normal work of woman in the world does not demand iron muscles, and the nervous equilibrium of sporting girls is often inferior to that of girls of a more feminine type, because the latter are better adjusted to their normal tasks. It is a very significant fact that Italian women, who are admittedly mothers of unusual excellence (feeding their babies well, and not liable to severe troubles in child-birth), are often, as girls, quite delicate and frail-looking, and totally unfitted for the violent activities of Anglo-Saxon girls. But it is the former and not the latter who are able to face with equanimity the pains and perils of maternity. Those who hail the pseudo-masculine girl of to-day as an advance on the softer type of womanhood are already suffering from a confusion of values. The truly feminine girl possesses a type of inner life different altogether from that of a boy. Masculine unemotionality would be a sign of ill-health in her case, because the normal woman is much more instinctive than the normal man, and reacts more swiftly to stimuli of the senses. Many famous actresses, women of immense vitality and power, have been given to fainting on the slightest provocation—not because they were weak, but just because their emotional life was exceptionally intense. A high degree of emotional susceptibility is not a sign of ill-health in a girl. It indicates that her essential femininity is strong, as it ought to be. Once we have got rid of the man-made standards which have conquered the educational world, the way is open to a true understanding of the question of hygiene for girls. Just as a boy is proud of his physical strength and hardihood, so should a girl be proud of her high sensibility and accompanying subtle intelligence. The great obstacle to be overcome is the all-pervading influence of the modern conception of sex equality, which denies to the feminine any value of its own and derives all standards from the male side of life.

It would be possible for me to occupy at least a hundred pages of this book with material demonstrating the injurious effects upon girls of the present mode of education. As I have already explained, the comparative success of girls in athletics proves nothing whatever. It remains to be seen what becomes of these girls in later life. Moreover, although we see and hear enough of the favourable side of the picture, there is something which almost amounts to a conspiracy of silence with regard to the other side. It is left to be filled in by those who have followed closely the future careers of the girls who throng our hockey fields and examination-rooms. There do not exist any definite statistics providing a reliable guide to the precise proportion of young women who break down in health in our modern establishments for the mental and physical masculinisation of women, but there is little doubt the number is very large. Within my own field of observation I have seen a proportion of more than 35 per cent. of serious breakdowns in health on the part of girls going in for higher education. Many of these have never recovered.[1]

Amongst doctors who have recently made a special study of the hygiene of the adolescent girl I may mention Stratz (Amsterdam), Menge (Heidelberg), and Sellheim (Tübingen). These are in agreement that, in the case of girls, general education should continue until the nineteenth year, when the nervous system has acquired increased stability. Before then, intense specialisation should not be permitted; and only those girls who are thoroughly fitted for it should be allowed to go forward to an academic career. In the general education it is desirable that a sound

[1] In Vienna (where the emancipation of women has made giant strides) the Press has recently drawn public attention to the abnormal increase of the death-rate amongst young women in the ages 18 to 28.

In Munich, Dr. Kaup (Professor of Hygiene) has warned parents and teachers that serious breakdowns in health frequently occur to the over-thin and overstrained sports girl of to-day.

The following extract is taken from a recent correspondence in the *Daily News* on the education of girls: "I have come very much into contact with young women just fresh from the secondary school, and they have seemed bright, happy, intelligent girls; nevertheless many of these promising girls have failed to make good in the race of life. They have suffered severely from overstrain. Out of about thirty girls whom I knew, several have suffered mental breakdowns, and others physical, while nine have died between the ages of eighteen and thirty."

In France, a committee representing leading medical opinion has brought pressure to bear upon the Government to control the athletics of girls in schools and colleges, so disastrous have been the results of over-athleticism.

Again, the English official Health Insurance figures show that illness is much more prevalent and costly amongst women-workers, especially the married women, than it is amongst the men. (See the *Journal of the Royal Statistical Society*, 1927, vol. iii, paper by Sir A. Watson.)

In *The Ethics of Feminism*, A. R. Wadia (Professor at the University of Mysore) writes (p. 60): "A quarter of a century of masculinised feminine education in India, especially in Bombay, has already witnessed a complete wreck of health among the school-going girls; and a very large proportion of lady graduates among Parsees have not survived the strain of childbirth."

D

training in domestic science and maternity work should be included.

Dr. J. W. Harms, who has studied adolescence from the standpoint of recent work upon the inner secretions (endocrinology), has come to the conclusion (in which he is supported by other workers in this important field) that the conditions of growth for the two sexes are so essentially different that, in order to bring our education into line with the indications of modern psychology, it would be necessary to remodel it radically, and to extend a much greater recognition to the reality of sex distinction. If girls are prepared for the same examinations as boys, it means that they are strained at the wrong growth-period. He draws attention to the fact that the existing system was developed with reference *to boyish needs only*. In the interests of the health of young women and with reference to the future of the race it is, he considers, "imperatively necessary" that we should establish a system of feminine education based upon a scientific knowledge of the psychology of girls. There should be special universities for women. If we fail to take these steps, the result is likely to be a progressive deterioration in the health of women.

. . . . .

The foregoing important problems are hardly ever considered in a serious and systematic fashion. Nothing could be more light-hearted than their treatment in the popular Press. Every now and then one comes across an article, written as a rule by some enthusiastic young feminist, explaining how easy it is to combine university training and subsequent professional life with an efficient discharge of feminine functions. But how seldom do we find even the faintest attempt to get at the exact truth with regard to the health and capacity of the modern girl student and professional woman, considered from the standpoint of racial interests!

We all know that a certain number of exceptionally energetic and able women do manage successfully to bring up a family of normal size after going through the entire treadmill of modern higher education and specialisation. The point is that the number is very small. It is so small that if this beneficent system were to be extended to cover the whole community, instead of being confined to a small section of society, it would practically exterminate the British race in some fifty or sixty years. Professor Stanley Hall showed, in extensive and painstaking researches into American conditions, that the number of children produced by women graduates had progressively diminished until it had (before the war) reached a figure that was simply infinitesimal, being less than one-quarter of a child per woman. In the British Isles things have not as yet quite reached this stage, although we are travelling at a smart pace along the same road. But here, too, the actual fertility of women graduates is excessively low. If we were to suppose an average of about one and a half children per marriage for the section of women graduates who marry (under 30 per cent.), we should be above the mark. This would give an average of less than half a child per graduate. No doubt many readers will be repelled by this cold-blooded calculation of the fertility of our most intellectual women, and it is not my intention to suggest that a woman's value can be measured by her physical fertility. It is, of course, true that much splendid work is done by spinster graduates. To this class belong many of the finest characters in our midst. But, while willingly admitting this, it remains true that the proportion of women graduates who make *racially* successful marriages is too low by far. If there is any truth whatever in the inheritance of ability, it is perilous, from a racial point of view, to train large numbers of our most brilliant feminine types (themselves members often of specially able families) to a life that means, in practice, an almost complete failure to make a normal contribution to the child-life of the future. ("Modern feminism is withdrawing more and more of the best women from marriage and motherhood." —Professor W. McDougall in *National Welfare and National Decay*.) It is specially important to lay weight upon this deplorable state of affairs in this chapter, since it is inseparably connected with the unpsychological education of girls (see also p. 227). It has been shown that the extreme infertility of the marriages of this type of woman is very largely voluntary, and is often occasioned by physical and nervous inability to face the task of maternity. And in those cases where the cause is not directly connected with the previous education, there is frequently an *indirect* connection, as when a married woman does not wish to be burdened with children because she has so many other interests and feels indisposed to spare the time and trouble to rear them (or more than one or two children). This is, after all, merely another form of unfitness for racial functions.

All these profoundly serious facts drive us to the conclusion that *the true type of education for women*, the type that shall give them a wide outlook and a rich and deep culture, without in any way unfitting them, psychologically or physically, for maternity, *has yet to be evolved*.

c. WOMEN AS MACHINES

The entire situation thus briefly outlined arises quite logically, almost inevitably, in fact, from the characteristics of the age in which we live. The two main tendencies of this age are *nationalism* and *industrialism*. Neither of these attaches the slightest importance to womanhood *as such*. To the militant nationalist, women seem indispensable in the sense in which Napoleon regarded them—as the mothers of numerous soldiers. To the industrialist, they appear useful as cheap labour, or as the potential mothers of cheap labour. But we may look in vain, in either direction, for any true valuation of woman *for her own sake*, for any appreciation of the unique cultural significance of the positively feminine aspect of reality. In this respect the world of to-day is far behind many a past age—this in spite of all that is said and written on the subject of the emancipation of woman, the golden age of womanhood, and so forth! Genuine positive feminism is, in fact, virtually bankrupt in the modern world. This true feminism stands for an independent valuation of such qualities as intuition, sensibility, devotion to persons, adaptability, gentleness, maternal instinct, passive endurance, sympathy, tact and diplomacy, swift insight into character, and profound interest in individuals. The materialism of the modern world has caused all such qualities as these to pass out of currency in the market of values. In their place we value highly all those characteristics which make for material success, e.g. vigour, independence, concentration, firmness of character, "push", hardness and hardiness, unemotionalism, egotism, business acumen, and so forth; and, more unconsciously than consciously, our girls' schools have become saturated with these values. If anyone doubts this statement, I invite him to test it by remarking to any ordinary English girl that she is as hardy as a boy. The girl will feel immensely flattered, thus showing to what an extent her mind has been captured by masculine values. If, on the other hand, he should say to the same girl that she was wonderfully feminine in her adaptability and quickness of insight, she would almost certainly feel more or less insulted.

Dr. Arabella Kenealy is unquestionably right in regarding

these symptoms of the age as evidences of spiritual and moral decline. The finer attributes of character are those which first disappear when a society moves downwards. The coarser qualities, such as physical strength or self-assertion, are the last to go, as they were the first to come. The inability of the modern industrialised world to appreciate the significance of sex distinctions and the value of the finer and more gracious feminine qualities is a mark of its superficiality, of its absorption in external things.

And, indeed, what value have they in such a world? There is certainly no reason at all why a young woman who is to spend all her days sitting in front of a typewriter or feeding pieces of tin-plate into a stamping machine should develop any of the richer attributes of humanity. She will be a more efficient Robot without them. What need has she for imagination, feeling, sympathy, intuition, or devotion? From the standpoint of practical efficiency, the present-day girls' school is right in concentrating on all that makes for material success. The trouble is, however, that deep down in the soul of the normal girl there dwell forces quite other than those which the school seeks to develop, emotions and dim instincts handed down from the remote past and now a part of the subconscious mind of the race. These rise in rebellion against the attempt to convert women into money-making machines, and their insurrection has important, and sometimes very disastrous, results for the life and happiness of the individual woman. General restlessness, nervous collapse, and sex hostility are closely connected with the attempt to force the development of the female sex along the lines of modern materialism.

The problem is much complicated by the plasticity of most young girls, which inclines them to accept the aims and ideals placed before them by their families or educators, although these may be, in reality, of a nature quite unsuitable for the girl's true development. Innumerable girls, once placed in the environment of the High School, with its cult of sport and preparation for professional life, allow themselves to be swept along by the suggestive influence which impinges upon them, and imagine that they will be perfectly happy if only they can be sent into this or that career, although in reality they may be quite lacking in any real gift for the type of work in question, and in their innermost selves—although they may not know it—are much more strongly inclined towards the traditional feminine side of life. But once launched into life as a bank clerk, a woman electrician, or what not, the girl, as she grows older and her subconscious life becomes stronger, finds that she is not satisfied in the grooves in which she must now run. Her more feminine personality, despised and neglected, begins to make its voice heard. Perhaps she has a breakdown in health. Perhaps she develops a strong sex hostility, and regards herself, or her sex in general, as suffering from male oppression. Perhaps she reads "advanced" literature and experiments in free love. Speaking broadly, these are all symptoms. The disease is *the fundamental maladaptation of the normal woman to the conditions of present-day civilisation*, with its total neglect of feminine psychology.

The oft-repeated saying that this is woman's great day, that now at last she has come into her own, is at once refuted by the obvious fact that women, and young women in particular, have never been so discontented as they are to-day. This rebellion of women is world-wide. But it reaches its maximum intensity in precisely those lands where the masculinisation of women has gone furthest. This is, of course, just what would be expected by anyone aware of the *real*, as distinct from the *alleged*, causes of the discontent. In America or in England, where women possess every conceivable right (except the right to be themselves!), the discontent is intense. In countries like Switzerland and Italy, where the rights are fewer, but where women have a far better chance to be women than in the Anglo-Saxon lands, there are few tokens of rebellion. The educated English girl of two generations ago had an 80 or 90 per cent. opportunity of marriage. This has now sunk to some 30 to 40 per cent. in the same class. Not for a moment do I suggest that all the modern girl wishes for is to be married. That she should wish to be independent rather than to be forced into an unsuitable marriage is wholly to her credit. But this does not alter the fact that women in the mass will not be permanently satisfied with a type of life which condemns them to life-long celibacy, nor will the transitory free-love unions recommended by advanced feminists prove satisfactory to any but a very small minority (leaving on one side the moral aspect of the matter).

The prevailing discontent is the best advertisement of the fact that we have not, as yet, found any effective solution of the problem of Woman and Society.

.   .   .   .   .

It was a profound misfortune for the Woman's Movement that it came upon the scene prior to the development of modern psychology. From the beginning, as we have seen, this whole current of thought stood under the powerful and in some ways very dangerous influence of Victorian rationalism and individualism, and in particular of the entirely unpsychological mode of thought of John Stuart Mill. But woman's problems are inextricably bound up with society as an organic whole. For their solution is required a knowledge of human nature, of psychology (social as well as individual), of sociology, of biology, and physiology. The method of the Mill school (the development of the individual as a unit, from a purely rational standpoint and without any reference at all to concrete psychological factors) is utterly inadequate when applied to these profoundly human problems. As a logician and as a stylist Mill was one of the greatest of Englishmen. As an inspirer of feminism his influence was unfortunate. If from the outset the Movement had been deepened and fructified by a close contact with modern psychology and sociology, its development would have taken place along far sounder lines. Consider the rich mine of information contained in the works of Stanley Hall, the encyclopædic studies of Havelock Ellis, the vast literature of the Freudian school (and of the daughter schools of Jung and Adler), the researches of the Eugenics Society, the recent work on sex psychology on the Continent (Eberhard, Moll, Möbius, Krafft-Ebbing, and others), and the important developments of child psychology. Had all these contributions had time to pour their united influence into the stream of feminist thought, it would have been deflected into quite another channel. The demand for sex equality (valuable as it is in some important respects) would have seemed quite inadequate. Even if pressed, the demand would have been supplemented by the much more important demand for a consideration of girls and women as specific beings, differing radically from men, and needing, for their ripe development, conditions other than those suitable for men. There might then have emerged *a specifically feminine view-point and life-philosophy, enabling feminism to enrich human life by bringing to bear fresh positive aims and characteristic influences.* In this way feminism would have worked towards a reform of civilisation, instead of becoming (as, in the main, it has become) a movement to adapt women to existing life along man-made lines.

CHAPTER IV

THE VICIOUS CIRCLE

The modern world is full of false ideas, crystallised into axioms. It is these conglomerations of error which, more than anything else, frustrate every attempt to reach a satisfactory solution of the problem of the modern girl and her relation to society.

The moment one opens a discussion of this burning question, one is met with the argument that England now contains an immense excess of women over men (largely a result of the war), and that, in consequence, it has become necessary to train the girls in the mass for independent careers. It is surprising how few people possess even the remotest knowledge of the actual statistical position.

The excess of women over men in the European lands is now much smaller than it was at almost any period during the last 500 or 600 years. In the fourteenth century the excess of women over men in Central Europe was about 15 per cent. For Frankfurt (Main) we have the following figures for the end of the century: population, about 10,000, composed of 4,600 men and 5,500 women—a much larger proportion of women than is to be found in Frankfurt to-day.

In modern England (with Wales) we have 18,500,000 males and 20,000,000 females (a ratio of 100 to 108). In present-day Germany there are 30,000,000 males and 32,500,000 females.

These figures speak for themselves. They reduce to a sheer absurdity the oft-repeated contention that there is now such an abnormal ratio between the sexes that our previous ideas as to woman's social functions must be revolutionised. If anything further were needed to knock this fallacy on the head it is to be found in the fact that nowhere do women pursue masculine careers more ardently than in America, where there is an excess of men over women.

Let us, then, dismiss from our minds the idea that there is any connection at all between the cult of independence and the pseudo-masculinism which, in practice, goes with it, and the numerical relationship between the sexes. As a matter of fact, the chief excess of women over men is to be found upon the higher age levels of the population. Consider the following figures for England and Wales, 1926:

Age Group.	Males.	Females.
15–20	1,800,000	1,790,000
20–25	1,680,000	1,740,000
25–30	1,405,000	1,655,000
30–35	1,300,000	1,570,000
35–40	1,240,000	1,470,000
40–45	1,225,000	1,425,000
45–50	1,170,000	1,330,000
50–60	1,990,000	2,160,000
60–70	1,185,000	1,355,000
70–80	500,000	680,000
80 and over	105,000	185,000

Here we see that under the age of twenty-five there is virtually no excess of females; there is, in fact, "a lad for every lass"!

In view of the gross inaccuracy of popular opinion on this matter, it is well to give the sharpest emphasis to the real state of things. It is quite common to hear well-educated people express the view that there are two women for every man in England. I recently met a cultured English-woman who firmly believed that not more than one woman in three could possibly marry, and it was only with the greatest difficulty that I could persuade her to accept the accuracy of the Governmental statistics.

In spite of the absurdity of these notions, there is no doubt whatever that they play a real part in determining the mental attitude of the nation towards the problem of the education of girls. The average person is fixed in the belief that, whereas 100 years ago it was possible for the great majority of women to marry, this is now out of the question, as there are "not enough men to go round". It is apparently held that all men are married, and the large body of unmarried women in our midst represent those who are "left on the shelf". Very few people know that there are well over two million unmarried men in the best marriageable ages.

The really decisive matter is not the ratio of men and women in the whole population, but the ratio during the marriageable ages. Consider the following figures for England and Wales (1926): Women of marriageable age (twenty to forty-five), about 7,900,000; men of marriageable age (twenty to fifty), about 8,000,000.

It is, of course, necessary to remember that men may, and often do, marry at a somewhat later age than women. In looking for a wife a man is practically confined to the age groups between twenty and forty (although, since a certain proportion of women over forty do marry, I have taken the groups up to forty-five into account); but a woman may very easily find a husband anywhere between twenty and fifty.[1]

[1] The German statistics throw a vivid light on the situation, proving conclusively that feminine celibacy is not due mainly to the excess of women over men, but to the non-marriage of so many men. Population: 62,500,000; males 30,200,000 and females 32,300,000. Men from twenty to forty-five—10,900,000, of whom *nearly* 5,000,000 *were unmarried*. Women from twenty to forty-five—12,600,000. Of every 100 women, about 58 are married (or widows). If all men married, this proportion would be 92.

Now, in the light of these figures, let us consider the remarkable fact that there are in this country some 3,000,000 unmarried women of marriageable age—most of them thinking, no doubt, that they belong to the army of the "superfluous".

We must, of course, allow for the women who simply do not wish to marry, or who have not found any suitable partner; but even then we cannot possibly account for the prodigious discrepancy between the number of women who *might* marry and those who *do*, save by assuming that there are some very powerful and unusual factors at work.

What are these factors?

There cannot be the slightest doubt that the general tendency of the present-day education of girls is largely responsible for the immense army of unmarried women in our midst. We cannot possibly divorce education from the rest of our national life. A machine which grinds out year by year hundreds of thousands of young women equipped solely with a view to competing with men in industry and business must of necessity create social conditions highly unfavourable to marriage and home-life. The struggle to earn a family wage or salary is thus made far more difficult for the average man. It would be impossible to form an estimate of the exact number of men who have been prevented from establishing homes of their own as a result of the competition of women, but it must be very large indeed. It has, for example, been reported in the daily Press that some hundreds of book-keepers, many of them married men with families to support, have recently been thrown out of work through their places being given to young girls who were content with a much smaller salary.

It is of considerable significance that the proportion of men amongst the unemployed should be so much larger than the proportion of women and girls (a short time ago

there were some five unemployed men for every female).
An inquiry by the Ministry of Labour into some 10,000
cases of persons drawing the "dole" showed that the
proportion of men was tending to increase, and that more
girls start work before the age of fifteen than was the case
four years ago. These are ominous indications, as they would
seem to point to a displacement of male labour by young
girls paid low wages. Moreover, with the ever-increasing
use of easily managed machinery, it would appear highly
probable that in the near future it will be more and more
practicable to employ girls rather than fully-paid men.

Without here going into the vexed question of equal pay,
it may be remarked, in passing, that even were this equality
achieved (and it is still far enough away), it would scarcely
apply as between quite young girls and men of twenty-one
and over. [It must, moreover, be remembered that the full
support of women workers for legislation on the lines of
equality of pay is problematical, since many of them realise
that they are employed just because they are cheaper. It
is more than likely that a demand for complete equality,
however beneficial it might be to men workers (through
reducing female competition), would be resisted by large
numbers of women and girl workers.] The Family Wage
System is referred to elsewhere (see p. 238), and I will only
remark here that it would be a matter of immense difficulty
to apply such a system so thoroughly as to abolish altogether
the handicap from which the employer of relatively highly-
paid family men suffers as compared with the employer of
cheap girl-labour.

It would be a fairly safe hypothesis to state that a considerable proportion, say at least a third, of the existing
army of bachelors are restrained from marriage, not through
any invincible repugnance to the married state, but from
economic reasons. The point is: How many of these men

have been prevented from "getting on", or even thrown into unemployment, through the competition of the host of women workers? To take a purely illustrative figure, if no more than some 750,000 of the men now unmarried were to be placed in such positions as to enable them to marry, we should at once withdraw from the labour market about a quarter of all our so-called "superfluous women", thus greatly relieving the tension of the existing situation.

In other words, even if the idea may seem strange to an age dominated by individualism, would it not be far more in the national interest to aim at reducing the mass of celibate women and building up the sinking domestic life of the country rather than to go forward with the existing plan by which we deliberately train battalions of young women to intensify the struggle of life for the young men of the nation, and at the same time for their own sisters?

.   .   .   .   .

The real trouble is that we are hopelessly entangled in *a vicious circle*. Parents and educators feel compelled—even in the face of their own better judgment—to give up the idea of training girls for their most natural career, marriage, and to fit them first and foremost for economic independence. The chance of marriage is uncertain, the expense of keeping girls at home too great, and, above all, the modern girl has set her heart upon "freedom". It is usually argued that if a girl can stand on her own feet she need not feel compelled to marry merely for the sake of having a home, but can afford to wait until she meets the right man; and, further, that she will be all the better for a thorough training in some profession. I will not deny that there is a germ of truth in this point of view. We do not wish to return to the time when young ladies stayed at home doing fine embroidery until they could catch a man. But none of these arguments, however true, can alter the logic of the situation. The fact remains that it is the flooding of the labour market with young women that has, more than anything else, lowered the chance of marriage for the modern girl; so that whereas sixty years ago a middle-class daughter could reckon on an 80 per cent. chance of marriage (at the least), the figure has now sunk to under 40 per cent. (in the case of university-trained women the marriage ratio is not more than some 25 per cent.).[1] We keep on moving round and round. Girls must earn their living because they cannot marry. Why cannot they marry? Because there are so many girls earning their living.

The present state of things is not an "act of God", the result of an unavoidable disparity between the sexes, but a problem capable of solution. It lies in our own hands to find some way of escape from the squirrel's cage. The whole matter is essentially a question of ideals—in fact, like most other things, it depends upon our ultimate beliefs. To those who have been converted to the ego-centric, utilitarian philosophy which reveals itself in much of the literature of feminism, everything I have just said will seem absurd. It will not move them in the least to know that some millions of girls have lost their chance of possessing a home of their own. Indeed, a well-known representative of left-wing feminism recently expressed her joy at the decline of marriage, since she held that it would open the door for irregular sex relationships, and thus assist in the "liberation of women".

On the other hand, to those who believe that marriage is the proper work of women, and that the sexes were intended to complement and aid each other, and not to cut each other's throats, it will seem of the very first importance to

[1] At the National Council of Women Conference at York (October 1928) it was stated by Lady Nunburnholme that: "Out of 644 medical women who have qualified in the last ten years, 15 per cent. have married, and of those 6 per cent. are still working."

remedy a state of things which imposes celibacy upon millions of women (over and above the numerically "superfluous" women).

It is true that some feminists—especially those of the left wing—have begun to realise that the economic emancipation of women is not all that was promised, that in practice it condemns masses of women to a drudgery no better than that from which they had thought to liberate themselves. Accordingly they have brought forward a remedy of their own—the union of marriage and professional life. It is proposed that wives and husbands should both pursue careers. In that way many of our bachelors, male and female, especially in the educated classes, will be able to marry.

There are a great many excellent arguments which might be advanced against this sort of home-life. But there is one which renders all the others superfluous. If this practice ever became at all general, it would be quite impossible to employ all the women who would be seeking careers. All the learned professions, and most of the other callings by which this army of would-be independent wives might hope to earn their bread, are already heavily overcrowded. What then would be the position (to consider only the higher social levels) if some million or more married women entered into the labour market? If all the married women in the country were to become infected with feminism, it would mean that we should have to find work for another 5,000,000 women. The plan is obviously absurd and impossible.

But if we once accept the idea that, for the great mass of wives (leaving out those who have some very special gift which would at once entitle them to make a footing), there can be no question whatever of economic independence, it follows plainly that all social developments likely to result in injury to the prospects of young men will rebound and hit the opposite sex with equal force. For this reason, if for no other, it is bad policy on the part of our feminine educators to ignore the results which must follow from training the large majority of girls to compete with (and often to undercut) men in every department of life.

These remarks must not be misunderstood. I in no way argue against the valuable woman worker, who, as doctor, lawyer, artist, or architect, may be doing good service to the community. We certainly need every ounce of ability we can get, male or female. But we must seek to reorganise our life so that wasteful competition shall be eliminated. It is anti-social to pour into already overcrowded fields of employment a stream of girls who have no special "call" there, but are merely sent into professional work because it is the fashion, or because they do not want to seem inferior to their brothers or boy friends. To the young man his success in life is a matter of life and death, whereas a very considerable fraction of his girl competitors are merely seeing life and amusing themselves for a year or two while they look round for a husband.

All social order must rest upon some kind of definition. If we entirely refuse to accept sex as the basic thing it obviously is, and thus fail to define the functions of men and women, there is nothing left for us but a chaotic state of society in which the sexes fight one another like dogs over a bone.

We must get back to the eternal truth that men and women are *complementary opposites*. Polarity is a law running through the universe, and it is the polarity of sex alone which enables civilisation to attain to its most harmonious development. Seek to do away with this fundamental distinction and duality of nature and function, and we sink into confusion.

The complexities of modern life have not essentially

altered the fact that man's primary function is to create
food and wealth for the community, while woman's primary
function is to bear and rear the children of the community.
Our modern doctrinaires have done their best to confuse
the distinction. What is the result? Millions of men without
work and millions of women without children!

.   .   .   .   .

If we consider the girls in any given school, it will be found,
looking ahead, that at least half of them will eventually
marry; yet, although this is well known, none of these girls
are actually educated with that object in view. Modern
parents and educators, even when they realise, as many of
them do, that marriage is the most important sphere of
work for a woman, almost always take the view that it is
useless to prepare any given girl for this life-work, since there
is no guarantee that she will actually marry. It is therefore
safer to train her for some paying career. The unfortunate
young woman of to-day is accordingly torn in two between
conflicting possibilities. No one feels certain that she is going
to have a home, therefore she is not trained for home-life.
On the other hand, the possibility that she will marry is just
strong enough to prevent her concentrating whole-heartedly
on her career. Her brother is, of course, spared this dis-
tressing conflict. Our modern educators seem incapable of
finding any way out of the muddle.[1]

[1] In her valuable work, *Das Seelenleben des Jugendlichen*, Dr. Charlotte
Bühler (Vienna) emphasises the frequency and importance of this
sort of conflict. The need of keeping two future possibilities in mind at
the same time adds greatly to the difficulties of development for the
modern girl. It confronts the girls' school of to-day with tasks that are
beyond it. The new world of facts and ideas seizes powerfully hold of
the mind of the adolescent girl; but she cannot, like her brother, transfer
the centre of gravity of her personality to this world (for any length of
time), for she all the while stands with one foot in another world of
personal relationships in which she is much more deeply rooted.

The root evil of the present system lies in its failure to recognise that a young woman's function in life is other than that of a young man, no matter if their paths do run for a while parallel.

Paternity plays a relatively small part in a man's life. It does not distract him from his work as a lawyer or an engineer—nay, it impels him to increased effort. But for the normal woman maternity remains the central fact of life. If there are communities to-day where this is not the case, where it is, in the phrase of one of our feminists, an "episodal occupation", it will be found that these are racially dying (one might take as an example Vienna, where an immense number of married women carry on professions, and where, save in the lowest social circles, the decline of population is very rapid).[1]

The boy of eighteen or nineteen can devote himself with a free mind to fitting himself for a career. To suppose that the budding young woman can do just the same is a fundamental error. Her whole mentality, with its deep-seated hereditary instincts, makes this almost impossible. To the young man the path towards racial fulfilment lies, in any case, through his profession. He knows that by "getting on" he draws nearer to founding a home. This is by no means true in the same sense for the young woman. In fact, in many lines of life, the greater the degree of specialisation by which she fits herself for her occupation, the poorer becomes her outlook as regards marriage and maternity. Judging by available statistics, the girl with no special training is more than twice as likely to marry as a highly-trained woman. It is obvious enough that this fact alone creates a vast difference as between boy and girl in their approach

[1] The present birth-rate in Vienna is 12·5 per 1,000; the death-rate is 13·75 per 1,000. But in the educated classes the former rate is far below the rate given for the whole city.

to modern life, and one far too little taken into consideration. It is common to read in popular expressions of opinion as to the education of girls that they will be enlarged in outlook through a thorough professional training, and will thus be enabled to tackle all the problems of marriage (should they marry) better; but it is seldom, or never, made clear that this very side-tracking of the girl into a career of this type reduces to an enormous extent her chance of marrying at all. In this department of life, as in so many others, it is very seldom possible to eat your cake and have it.

From this root evil there flows a train of serious consequences. The average modern girl is totally unprepared for marriage and its responsibilities. If she succeeds, it is probably by instinct; it is in spite of her education rather than because of it. She spends the years, say from seventeen to the early twenties, in training as a chemist, secretary, teacher, or what not. But her knowledge of typewriting, Latin, or the derivatives of benzol, will not be of much use in the by no means easy task of running a home on a small income.

In practice it amounts to this: the schools regard marriage as something of altogether secondary importance, and concentrate mainly (but not quite thoroughly) on professional training, the girl being all the time handicapped more or less by home duties from which the boy is free. The whole position is profoundly unsatisfactory. Marriage is not a matter of secondary importance for the nation, however much the schools may push it into the background. It is as important for the nation to possess well-trained wives and mothers as it is for it to possess efficient sailors or engineers. It is more difficult to run a home really competently than to sail a ship or manage a machine. On every hand we find mothers complaining that the modern school totally unfits their daughters for home-life.

The full absurdity of the situation stands out sharply

when we imagine a reversal of the sexes. Let us assume that in a certain school most of the boys will go into the Navy— at least, it is not quite *certain* that they will, it is merely *probable*. The parents would then say: "Well, it is no use training our boys for the Navy, because we are not sure that they will ever go to sea. We will have them all trained as tailors and carpenters, and then we shall be on the safe side. If, after all, they do join the Navy, it will be useful for them to know a trade." Let us suppose, further, that some 60 per cent. of these boys do really enter the Navy on leaving school. They would then be entirely without the preliminary experience and training which is essential to make a success-ful seaman, and would find themselves hopelessly handi-capped by comparison with other boys who had been sent to a proper naval school. What would people say about this system? And what would happen to the Navy? And what *is* happening to the domestic life of the Anglo-Saxon race? It is the same tale wherever the English tongue is spoken— more hotels, fewer homes; more divorces, fewer children.

Arguing thus, I do not, however, deny that there is great weight in the arguments of those who say that in the world as it is now it is quite impracticable to train girls for marriage. From the standpoint of immediate expediency the parents of daughters can hardly be expected to take any other view. But this does not lift us out of the rut. If the modern system is, speaking racially, a cul-de-sac, it is small comfort to be told that we cannot go along any other road. We are here confronted with a problem which goes far deeper than any mere reform of educational ideals or methods.

As we saw in the first chapter, the emancipation of women has created problems which cannot be solved along the paths which we are now travelling. The problems touched upon here take us outside the scope of our subject (in the narrower sense) and lead us to a reconsideration of the ideals at the basis of our civilisation. Upon the ground of the existing moral and cultural ideals it is indeed difficult to see how we can leave the cul-de-sac and return to the highway of life. In the next chapter we shall consider very briefly one or two points of view of fundamental importance with a view to clarifying the situation.[1]

[1] Some portions of this chapter appeared in *The Nineteenth Century and After* (July 1928), and I am indebted to the kindness of the Editor for permission to make use of them here.

CHAPTER V

THE ORGANIC VIEW OF SOCIETY

It will be necessary to leave a fuller consideration of woman's social functions (which in their turn give us the true goal for the education of girls) to a later section of this work. But it will not be out of place to deal, in passing, with certain basic questions suggested by the foregoing chapters.

In reality, the individualistic doctrines which have all along been so influential in the Woman's Movement (especially in its relation to education) are now out of date. Yet, by virtue of its momentum, the educational machine still runs on in the grooves which were laid down before the commencement of the present century. There is astonishingly little contact between the data of modern psychology and the presuppositions which guide and inspire our educators.

It is my contention that we have still to do for girls' schools what was done for boys' schools a hundred and more years ago—done, it is true, more by instinct and common sense, or by tradition, than by any systematic psychological study—namely, to model them upon a sound knowledge of the mentality and instincts of their pupils.

The general tendency of modern philosophy is away from the atomism and individualism of the Victorian utilitarians, and in the direction of viewing reality in such a fashion that the different component parts acquire their significance through their relation to a larger synthesis. The separate unit is not to be understood as a unit, but only through its organic connection with a whole larger than itself. Thus regarded, differences of structure and capacity become part of a scheme in which every difference has a purpose, and all the differences possess an organic relation to the whole.

The utilitarian-mechanical view of life sees the various units which make up reality as so many detached parts, in no sense inwardly related; the organic view perceives a meaning *immanent* in every part, a meaning that does not become clear until we know something of the whole.

It will be clear that the first view, the mechanical, works against any deeper understanding of the significance of sex difference; while the latter attaches a profound teleological significance to all differences of structure, such as sex. From the former standpoint, woman will seem an isolated unit, side by side with man, also an isolated unit; from the latter, the real meaning of womanhood will become apparent only when we consider woman in relation to the human race as a whole, of which the two sexes are component and complementary parts.[1]

The various problems centring about sex and education are greatly simplified when envisaged from this organic standpoint. Society, considered as an evolving process, is the larger whole from which is derived the synthesis giving us the function of each sex. True sex equality thus follows quite naturally. It must depend upon the complementary relation of man and woman, and not upon sex homogeneity or similarity. The sexes are seen to be so related that neither can perform the functions of the other, while their essential interdependence entirely excludes all crude ideas of superiority or inferiority.

[1] Cf. *The Psychology of Society*, by Mr. Morris Ginsberg, chap. iv. Speaking of the conflict between the social and individual schools of psychology, the author says: "From the controversies between the opposed schools we do learn at any rate this much, that individuals are intrinsically and essentially related to one another, and that society is not an artificial product, a mere mechanical contrivance to hold together a mass of individuals conceived as capable of existing in the fullness of their being in isolation."

The true orientation of the education of girls is accordingly derived from a study of their social functions—such as maternity, the maintenance of home-life in general, the cultivation of social life, the care of national health and hygiene, medical work, children's welfare work, the development of various special fields of work in which women are gifted (the drama, art, music, architecture, handwork, artistic dressmaking, and so forth).

It is not, however, implied for a moment that women should be forcibly debarred from an entry into any other spheres of work. If a given girl specially desires to become a barrister, an engineer, or an aviator, let her follow this line, and let the door be kept open. But—*and this is the main point*—it must never be regarded as *normal* that a girl should enter into such spheres of work; and, above all, girls' schools must not be run in the interests of these more exceptional girls. In the first place we must set the work and ideals of those girls who are to pursue the normal line of function, and only as exceptions should we train a few specially gifted girls for professions which in their nature are not adapted to the average feminine physique or mentality. There could be no greater error than to allow the mass of girls to be deflected from their natural interests because a small minority of girls have special wishes in other directions.

The general re-orientation of our educational outlook which would come about in accordance with the line of thought here suggested would, it is clear, be such as to assign an increased importance to the psychological and particular. Girls would be educated along the lines indicated by their own particular qualities, and by the relationship which these bear to the purpose of society as a whole. The girl would no longer be regarded (as is now far too much the case) as an isolated autonomous unit, but as a member of the whole. To this whole each part owes the duties it is best able to render in accordance with its own specific gifts.

This may be described as the functional view of education, in contrast to the utilitarian, autonomous view. Seen from the former standpoint, life possesses an inner meaning, and each unit has a part to play in the development of this meaning. Viewed from the latter, life has no meaning; it is no more than a field of conflict where separate units meet, each bent on its own ends. The functionalist sees life as an organic whole, and not from the standpoint of abstract ideas, such as freedom or equality (although the significance of these within the whole cannot be denied). Each member of the whole has functions to discharge which make it equal to every other member, since all are interdependent parts. The heart is equal to the brain, because both must function properly in order that the body may live. But this equality is something quite other than an equality based upon similarity of function. If the heart were to imitate the brain in its structure or working the body would die.

The problem is to create an educational system for girls which, in general tendency, will be true to the distinctive character of woman, while being sufficiently elastic to permit of a minority being trained along specialist lines where this is advisable. But let us avoid the fatal error of allowing the spirit of narrow masculine specialisation to colour the education of women in general, as is now too largely the case.

We should seek to develop feminine types so strongly marked and so self-confident in their femininity that *they can cry halt to the spread of man-made ideals and life standards*, and work against the disastrous mechanisation and de-personalisation of modern life. Much would be gained if we could intensify sex magnetism and the polarity of sex, thus averting the serious impoverishment of life and culture which results from the levelling down of sex differences.

. . . . .

The fundamental weakness of modern Western civilisation is the lack of an adequate, positive philosophy of life. In its absence life disintegrates into a pure chaos of opinions. Where such a philosophy exists, men and women see reality as a whole, and each particular sphere of human activity falls into its natural place within the whole. The feminine side of life does not seem less significant than the masculine, since both are equally essential to the existence and progress of society. *Sub specie æternitatis*, a woman nursing a child is in every respect equal to a man writing a book on conic sections! If there were no babies, what, indeed, would be the use of conic sections or of anything else?

As it happens, the world of to-day is still under the influence of a one-sided rationalism and materialism, a valuation of life which attaches first importance to the technical, impersonal, and external aspects of reality, while neglecting the emotional, personal, and spiritual elements in our existence. Since the peculiar strength of woman's nature lies just precisely in the world of the emotional, human, and spiritual, it need not surprise us if the modern woman, finding herself in a world which despises all that she instinctively holds dear, and being thus made to feel inferior, seeks refuge in a determined attempt to assimilate the prevailing masculine mode of life and thought, even though in so doing she leaves the best of herself behind.

In *Social Evolution* Benjamin Kidd demonstrated, with an imposing wealth of argument, that a social system based upon the rational and practical is doomed to decay. The world of the emotional, subconscious and irrational, of the mystical and spiritual, is not merely decorative, it is essential to the continued existence of the human race. In its absence the springs of life run dry and our vitality withers away. Elsewhere I endeavour to make it clear that it is woman's specific task not only to preserve the race in a physical sense, but also to keep alive and at full strength all those irrational and imponderable life-elements which, while not appealing to the technical-practical mentality of to-day, are in reality basic for the whole of civilisation. For this purpose, however, we need *real* women, not imitation men.

.   .   .   .   .

With the transference of interest to the psychological side of life, fresh perspectives have opened out before us. It is now realised that human personality is immeasurably deeper and more complex than was formerly supposed, that it contains a whole world of subconscious instincts and emotions, the true significance of which was barely suspected in the days of Mill and his school.

The Woman Question can never again assume the simple form which it possessed in the eyes of the doctrinaire rationalists. In woman we now perceive an incarnation of elemental life-impulses of a decisively different kind from those which animate the opposite sex, and the place which woman will take in the society of the future (shaped as it must be with reference to a deeper conception of personality) will depend upon a riper knowledge of these psychological realities, rather than upon abstract doctrines. The answer to the question, Where is woman going, and what should she do? is to be sought *within the soul of woman herself*, and not in the teachings of an intellectualism divorced from concrete reality.

CHAPTER VI

TOWARDS SEX EQUALITY

(a) WHAT IS SEX EQUALITY?

THE controversy which rages to-day over the sex equality question is carried on without either side taking breath long enough to attempt an accurate definition of terms. Yet the precise meaning of the terms employed is of decisive importance. In the absence of clear thinking upon this matter we find ourselves dependent upon vague and stupid catchwords.

A logical examination of what is really involved in the equality discussion reveals depths and complications not apparent on the surface. We then see that sex equality is a difficult problem, and not something which can be established overnight by Act of Parliament.

How many people have troubled to ask themselves in just exactly what sense are the sexes presumed equal? They are not equal physically, since the organic differences between the sexes are obvious and irremovable. It is idle to suppose that any amount of training will ever make women in the mass as strong as men in sheer physique.[1] Are they equal mentally? It is impossible to maintain that entities which are organically different can be identical mentally, unless we are prepared to argue that mind and body have no connection—a position which is quite untenable.

It may be said that by equality we do not mean *identity* (or even similarity), that women may be quite equal to men,

---

[1] The energy and comparative success of the sporting girl of to-day must not be allowed to blind us to the fact that a wide gap separates eminine achievements in this field from those of the opposite sex. Even the best women tennis-players, for example, cannot play on level terms against men of their own category.

although less strong physically and of another mentality. Now we are on the right track. We are beginning to see that equality cannot mean homogeneity, and something has been gained. But the thoughtless catch phrases which are current to-day do not even embody this much of truth, since they are very frequently used as if equality *did* mean homogeneity, as if men and women were equal in the downright sense of being in all respects the same in their capacity and mentality. The truth of the matter is that those who most often employ the phrase "sex equality" cannot rid themselves of the feeling that inequality must mean inferiority on the part of women. Every attempt to throw light upon the actual differences between men and women is furiously resisted, under the belief that it conceals some sinister purpose tending towards the enslavement of women. It is therefore important to emphasise sharply that no such purpose lies behind this chapter. It is written solely with the object of elucidating a very complex matter and ridding the atmosphere of a few of the prejudices and errors with which it is thick.

At the very outset let us be clear on the point that equality cannot mean homogeneity. It can only mean that woman's life and work is not less valuable than man's.

The assertion of women's rights would be strengthened, and not weakened, if the propaganda were to be purified from the muddle-headedness which results from a failure to analyse the implications of equality as between beings with different functions. Phrases such as "complete equality of opportunity " are nonsense. They possess no definite meaning. The functions of the sexes are not interchangeable. How then is full equality, in this sense, possible? Men cannot be mothers. They are therefore deprived for ever of one of the greatest of human opportunities, of an experience different from fatherhood, and, in a human sense, far

deeper, richer, and more thrilling. Similarly, speaking generally, women cannot be sailors (although an isolated woman
may succeed as a sailor), and are in their turn deprived of an
interesting experience.[1]

.   .   .   .   .

In England and America, at any rate, these logical
distinctions do not carry any weight. The aim of the average
feminist is purely practical. But the danger of the Anglo-
Saxon method of moving slowly from precedent to precedent,
without being guided by any fundamental theory or having

[1] One of the profoundest and most sensitive studies of the sex equality
question to be found in modern literature is the article "Die Wertfrage
zwischen den Geschlechtern" (*Zeitschrift für Menschenkunde*, May 1926),
by the well-known German writer on psychology and social subjects,
Oskar A. H. Schmitz, who takes up the standpoint that the polarity
of man and woman is a metaphysical principle essential to the stability
of all human society, and containing in itself the idea of equality, since
neither is, in an ultimate sense, independent of the other. "The human
race would not have appeared upon earth in two sexes unless each of
the two forms had to express a meaning of its own. People may deny
this differentiation of sex, since it is not possible to reduce it to a formula,
but reality will not be mocked. . . . The confusion which to-day
reigns in respect of sex equality has been brought about by those who
no longer feel quite sure that they really are equal; in other words,
by women who are no longer fully self-confident as *women*, but who have
fallen under the spell of masculine suggestion, and are painfully anxious
to demonstrate that women are just as capable as men of producing
achievements of the masculine type, because they are firmly convinced
in their own minds that what is womanly can never be as valuable
as that which is manly. . . . It is essential that, transcending the
conflict, we should seek to win a new insight into the meaning of the
two forms of humanity, man and woman; not with the reactionary
purpose of depriving women of any of their painfully won rights, but
in the hope that women will, through a realisation of their nature (and
many have already attained to this standpoint), again desire of their
own free will to be women, although the possibility of following the
opposite path is open to them. . . . The problem of equality becomes
hopelessly muddled if we measure women against men, instead of by
their own standards." In a work entitled *Wespennester* (vol. i, pt. 2)
Schmitz has recently still further developed his ideas.

any definitely envisaged goal, is that we may drift into quite unforeseen situations. It is certainly perilous to be too rigidly logical; but it may, in the long run, be no less dangerous to dispense altogether with logic.

We see this danger clearly in the demand for a sex equality which remains wholly undefined in its nature.

That great mass of people who support the Woman's Emancipation Movement is composed of many elements, who, if put to it to define their positions, would reveal themselves as differing very widely indeed in their aims. Some are orthodox and conventional; some are advocates of "free love"; some favour birth-control; others are bitterly opposed to it; some stand on the doctrinaire basis of sex homogeneity; while others admit a wide difference of nature and function between the sexes. But they are all at one in demanding for women enlarged opportunities of life, and for the purpose of their campaign this demand has been crystallised in the phrase "equality of opportunity", or simply "sex equality". The fight for this "equality" goes on, although no one knows exactly what it means or where it will take us.

Those who follow the Feminist Movement in its social and political activities will realise that what is involved, in practice, by equality of the sexes, is simply that wherever a door is shut it should be opened. If some body of men—such as the ministry—does not admit women, then it is demanded in the name of equality that they should be admitted. Men being taxi-drivers, a whoop of delight goes up in the camp of the equalitarians when some enterprising girl becomes a taxi-driver. And so on. This kind of "feminism" should be called *masculinism*, for it consists simply in the imitation of men.

When we come to another field of life, that of the feminine functions proper, we find that most (although, in justice,

F

I admit not *all*) feminists change their ground very swiftly. We hear no more of sex equality or the imitation of men. The object now is to gain for women every possible advantage. For example, many feminists have supported laws compelling the fathers of illegitimate children to pay for their maintenance—a position which could not be deduced from any theory of sex equality, but is based upon the old-fashioned view that a man is more responsible than a woman in the sphere of sex. In America feminists have gone to a great length in demanding for married women all sorts of privileges and advantages which have nothing to do with sex equality, but which, on the contrary, give to the wife a legal standing superior to that of the husband (see p. 116).

Now it is true that there are some really logical feminists who wish to have sex equality in this field too, and are even prepared to urge that all married women should be self-dependent, that they should dispense entirely with all legislation protecting wives and giving them a status of legal privilege.[1] But this school has very little real influence,

[1] For example, Mrs. Billington Greig (one of the most prominent of the suffragettes) said: "The new demands, for civic equality, and the old condition (i.e. protection and maintenance) cannot subsist together. But the abolition of the old condition must place upon the women who make the new demands a very heavy burden—the burden of *personal* economic independence" (quoted by Mr. Harold Owen in the *Evening News* of October 28, 1927). This is certainly the logic of the case. But, as we all know, there is little connection between politics and logic. As a matter of fact, women have now received their civic equality. But there is not the slightest likelihood that the average wife will become economically independent, whatever Mrs. Greig or any other feminist may say or not say. Another feminist is also quoted by Mr. Owen, as follows: "Equality forces her (the modern woman) to be self-supporting—anything less makes her equality an imposture. And when woman is self-supporting, with all the consequences, the whole edifice of life-marriage will fall to the ground." Such views represent the standpoint of the really consistent and fair-minded feminists, who see that men cannot reasonably be expected to support women who do not recognise any marital authority. The point is that

and there is no probability that its views will ever actually prevail in our laws and social practice. Let the reader mark these views do not prevail (nor would those who wish to preserve monogamy desire to see their prevalence), and in consequence the modern man finds himself in the impossible position of being required to maintain a person over whose conduct and movements he has no control whatever. In the same article Mr. Owen quotes his own opinion, expressed five years before the vote was granted: "Woman will secure her political power on the ground of her natural 'equality', and will retain all her privileges on the ground of her natural 'weakness'." And this is exactly what has happened.

One of the most recent expositions of left-wing feminism is Mrs. Bertrand Russell's *Hypatia*, which frankly repudiates monogamy, on the ground that free women cannot be bound: "As a Labour Minister is corrupted by Court dress, so is a free woman by the marriage contract. Nothing but our desire for children would make us endure it." An easily dissolved form of sex union, with no compulsion on either side, and the State support of maternity, is part of her programme. Even if we accept the view of the authoress of *Hypatia* that monogamy has no moral significance, the fact remains that there is not the slightest practical outlook in this direction. No one could possibly suppose that we shall see the abolition of monogamy within measurable time in England. In effect, Mrs. Russell, and those who think with her, ask men to give up all the rights which they still enjoy under the marriage contract, under the plea that a free union is better than one in which there is compulsion; but while themselves claiming immediately the most complete freedom, the husband must be content with the vague promise of a new form of marriage at some unspecified date in the future—perhaps in a hundred years or more. In the meantime he must continue to shoulder all the traditional burdens of marriage. Even in Russia, where left-wing feminist ideas have been to some extent realised (as regards ease of divorce), the husband is still legally responsible for the children. It is, as a matter of fact, virtually impossible to place the whole burden of supporting families upon the State. The actual situation is that, while men have granted many of the demands of the feminists, they have done so without taking any precautions to see that the concessions promised on the feminist side have materialised.

Nothing is so characteristic of nearly all feminists of this school as their quite unconscious, and often almost comical, obliviousness of the masculine view-point. It seems to them so natural that life should be arranged wholly from the standpoint of female interests, that they have never troubled to imagine what life looks like as seen through masculine spectacles.

well that what is *actually* taking place (although it is not postulated in theory) is that *women are advancing rapidly into all the fields of masculine work, under the battle-cry "sex equality"; but, at the same time, are not giving up, but rather consolidating and strengthening, all their special sex privileges in the field of function.*

Not for a moment is it alleged that feminists as a body are insincere. But the facts of nature are too much for them. They may be equalitarians, but they are at the same time women. On the one hand they are genuinely anxious to secure for women equal opportunities in the world of work, but on the other they cannot bring themselves to take the heroic step of dropping the valuable legal and social privileges which Western civilisation has granted to women in the world of function. It is only necessary to read a little of its literature to see that the Woman's Movement has, all along, been in a muddle with regard to sex questions. Its leaders and publicists are committed to the belief that there is nothing in woman which places her either above or below man, yet their own instincts as women (and in some cases mothers) prompts them to attach a special importance and sanctity to maternity, of a kind quite incompatible with matter-of-fact sex equality. Reading between the lines, it is easy to perceive that not a few feminist writers are much more enamoured of the matriarchal social state than they are of the sex equality ideal. Dr. Alice Stockham, for example, takes a romantic and idealistic view of woman's functions which makes nonsense of the idea of sex equality; and in one of the chief text-books of feminism, Mrs. Gilman's *Women and Economics*, the matriarchal ideal comes strongly to expression. Again, in Mrs. Bertrand Russell's *Hypatia* it is fairly obvious that the idea of sex equality has receded into the background, if it has not been totally abandoned.

The Women's Emancipation Movement has all along

drawn its strength from opposition. In revolt, it is not necessary to define one's own position, as long as there are good grievances to serve as weapons; but once the uphill path of reconstruction is reached, it soon becomes impossible to get on without unity and clarity of purpose. *We have now come to a stage when it is impossible to evade the task of analysis and definition.* This short study of the equality problem will have served a good purpose if it does no more than attract attention to its pitfalls and complications.

b. Woman's Two Worlds

For a moment let us return to *Woman and Labour,* a work which may still be reckoned as the leading text-book of feminism. Here we find Olive Schreiner endeavouring, in rather an ingenious way, to evade the problem of sex equality by dividing life into two compartments: "a very narrow but important region" (she is referring to the racial side of life), where she admits that the difference of functions between men and women is not to be escaped; and "the large fields" of life in which sex function plays no part at all, as she supposes. (See the section entitled "Sex Differences".)

Now could anything be more misleading than this division of life into two fields, one narrow and the other large? It is clear enough that the large fields are dependent upon the smaller one, because our entire civilization rests upon the home and upon maternity. The other spheres (by which the authoress means work in general—art, science, trade, the professions, etc.) are, although wider in area, not in reality independent of the field in which race function is admitted. It is not so much a case of two departments of life as of a substructure and a superstructure of life. There are no such departments. It is a psychological impossibility for a woman

to keep her sex solely for the racial sphere and then in her
ordinary life to have no sex. We have to deal here, simply and
solely, with an attempt to solve the equality problem along
all-too-simple lines by minimising, most unwarrantably, the
importance of those aspects of life in which even the feminist
must admit that sex counts. As a corollary of this false view
we find the belief that maternity is no more than a sort of
"side-line" which a woman can carry on parallel with her
activities as a professional worker.

In this way it is perhaps possible to make out a case for
sex equality (in the crude sense, as distinct from genuine
sex equality based upon the recognition of functional
difference), namely, by assuming that men and women do
not differ in their mental qualities, and that the side of life
where they do differ is "narrow" and does not influence the
wider side of life. But, as will be evident to all those who
read further in this book, such a case rests upon a whole
series of fundamental errors and misconceptions, and Nature
will take a revenge upon those whose life-philosophy is so
out of keeping with her laws.

But even if we were to grant, for the sake of argument,
that it *were* possible to divide life into these two fields, the
case we have considered would still be unsound. If it were
feasible for women to obtain a position of complete equality
in the field of work (which is still very far from being
achieved), it would still be quite impossible to establish
sex equality in the realm of function. For the home is
woman's own special field, in a sense quite other than it
could ever be man's field, however much men may be
domesticated. Here women have reigned from time immemorial, and will continue to reign. Those who do not understand the reason for this are past argument. It is a fact
conditioned by the psychology of woman herself and by all
the traditions of European social life. The man may, of

course, play his part as a father side by side with the mother. But in ninety cases out of a hundred the influence of the father is nothing in comparison with the influence of the mother. For the latter is not influence, but something far more fundamental and primitive. If we remember that the Jesuits maintain that, given a child until the sixth year, they can mould his whole future, we shall be less likely to underrate the all-determining power of women over the life of the nation, holding in their keeping, as they do, the whole infant life of the people during the most impressionable years. How misleading, then, is the attempt to represent this influence as but an equal fraction of a narrow field of our life! It is a sober statement of irrefutable fact to say that woman, in her rôle as wife and mother, holds the fate of the nation in the hollow of her hand. The effort of the feminists to brand those who hold this view as sentimentalists, and thereby to discredit them in the view of the public by scoffing references to "the hand that rocks the cradle rules the world", is but their method of evading an argument which, if accepted, would invalidate their position. If we are realistic enough to see clearly how enormous is the power of woman in the home, we must, if we are at all logical, take this power into account in reckoning up the balance between the sexes. We can no longer allow this aspect of the problem to be pushed into the background.

To express the matter somewhat differently, *woman has two worlds*—the world of maternity and home-life and the world of outside work. Her influence in one of these is unique and decisive, and will remain so, no matter what alterations may take place in law or theory. Man exerts his power (speaking broadly) in the latter world, and not in the former. Even in countries like India, where the standing of the husband is legally and theoretically much higher than that of the wife, the actual power wielded by the wife and

mother is immense. The man's authority is something
formal and external, but the real ruler of the home is the
mother. Woman's natural power as the creator of life and
the educator of the infant is in fact indestructible, and is
often strongest when it is least emphasised in law. The position of women in France or Italy is outwardly lower than in
England, but in practice the mother of a family, in either
Latin land, is in a position of such dominance that her
authority over her children extends to (and even beyond)
the time when they are middle-aged men and women and
themselves parents.

It is therefore superfluous to labour the point that if
women were ever to attain to a position of full equality in
the external world of business, industry, politics, and the
professions, the resulting social system would *not* be one
embodying sex equality. For nothing can destroy the unique
authority and influence of women in the other world, that
of sex function.

To make my contention perfectly clear, let us imagine a
system of points granted in proportion to influence. We
might assign, for example, 50 points to the world of economic
life, politics, and so forth, and another 50 to the world of
sex and the family (with infant education and nursing).
Supposing women to have attained equality in the first
field, they would obtain here 25 units of influence, the other
25 going to the males. But in the second field, the women
would take at least 40 units for themselves. *On the balance,*
65 units of power would go to the women of the community and
35 to the men.

The actual situation thus represents not so much an
approach towards sex equality as a gradual drift towards a
species of modern matriarchy. So long as men hold a pre-
dominating position in the world of business, politics, and
the sciences and arts, this matriarchy is still far enough

away. But it is important that we should see the situation
for what it is, and realise that were a state of full sex equality
in the external world (industry, politics, and so on) ever
realised, the women of the community would be in a commanding position on the balance. They would be man's
equals in man's own traditional world, while at the same
time reigning supreme in another world of their own, free
from all masculine competition.

.   .   .   .   .

To the reader who has followed the earlier section of this
book, it will be clear that this situation has arisen not so
much from any deliberate desire on the part of women to
win a position of social dominance, but in consequence of
their own philosophy of individualism and masculinism.
Most feminists underrate the value of woman's work as
woman, while overrating the importance of all masculine
activities. It has thus seemed to them that the very essence
of the equality problem must lie in women equalling men
in men's work, and they have tended to regard the advantages possessed by women in virtue of their sex as being of
little significance. It is just here that we see how unrealistic
and doctrinaire is the entire feminist life-philosophy. In
actual life we all know how enormous is the power of women
in all those relationships where the erotic factor plays a
part, and no solution of the equality problem which does
not take this fully into account is worth the paper it is
written on. There are scarcely any limits to the influence
that a clever and attractive young woman can wield over
the men who come within her radius; and that is especially
the case to-day, when men are prevented by the established
code of manners from making any use of those more aggressive personal qualities which are often found in their sex.
In the Anglo-Saxon lands, more particularly, the average

man is compelled to submit to a code of social conduct which gives women an almost complete mastery in every sort of personal relation. Joan rings up her friend Jack and says: "Hullo, old thing! I want you to take me to the dance at the Hotel Imperial to-night. Mind you come at eight-thirty sharp!" And if Jack desires to be thought a "good sport", he has no alternative but to obey the command. Nothing is more characteristic of the *camaraderie* which exists in present-day England between young people than the fact that the girl takes the leadership from beginning to end. The man is little more than a tool in the hands of his girl friend. After all, what can the poor fellow do? Rigid conformity to the established code is the guiding rule of school and college in all Anglo-Saxon countries. Once this code has ruled that women must give the lead, the typical product of the public school and university will always follow the ruling. There is nothing the young Englishman fears so much as the charge of not showing "good form". If the young man should rebel, he can always be cowed into obedience by the terrible phrase, "Oh, Jack! I thought you were a gentleman!" Thus, in the twinkling of an eye, the ground is shifted—equality is dropped, and the idea of chivalry is brought into action. The great majority of English girls may be too "nice", too good-natured and unspoiled to abuse their power in any serious way; but the consequences to the man's character of his state of subordination are injurious. It deprives him of the very wholesome feeling of responsibility. Further, granted a girl who is of a selfishly dominating disposition, or worse still, one who is a real "minx", it is very easy indeed for a young Englishman to drift into situations full of danger for his future life. A girl of nineteen or twenty is some five years older than a boy of the same age. In knowledge of life and in erotic development she is a woman, while he is no more than a half-baked man. When we add to this situation the strong love of power over persons which is one of the characteristics of womanhood, we are able to form some conception of the incalculable influence of women in England. The power wielded through the ballot-box or in the professions is nothing in comparison with the power which girls exert through their sex.[1]

This power is still further enhanced by reason of the peculiar type of masculinity which is developed through the education and tradition of the educated classes in England. The form-giving type of man, the ideal of the public school and college, is the easygoing, sporting, breezy, gentlemanly sort of fellow, the man with pleasant manners and a knack of wearing his clothes well. He is a good player of games and a good soldier. But he is lamentably lacking in intellectuality and initiative. In all things he is the slave of tradition and environment.

The modern girl rather likes this sort of boy as a friend, but in her heart she despises him. She is herself so superior to him in realism and grasp of life that she cannot help feeling that he is something rather less than her equal. She misses in him, above all, the *distinctive* sex qualities, just

---

[1] By way of comment on this state of things, I quote from Mr. Goldring's novel *The Façade* (a study of modern love relationships amongst the educated classes):

"I am not saying anything against the modern emancipated young woman. In many ways she is admirable. She is an excellent companion; she is too self-respecting, as a rule, to let men spend too much money on her; she makes, in short, a charming *hetaira*. She has fought for and gained her 'right to be happy'. She is sexually free, or thinks she is, and has achieved *something more than mere equality with the male*. At the present time, comparing her with the sexless young men of her own age, *she is dominant. . . .*" (The italics are mine.)

In *The Revolt of Youth*, by Judge Lindsay, we are told that the girl plays a completely dominating part in the friendships and temporary sex connections which form such a feature of American life amongst students and young people in business and professional life.

those qualities that a woman instinctively looks for in a man. The natural woman expects to find in her mate a higher degree of initiative and intellectuality than she herself possesses. She at once respects a man who can show these qualities. In her subconscious mind the woman does not really want a pleasant companion who is nothing more.

.   .   .   .   .

Having thus briefly indicated that women do really possess a large area of influence not enjoyed by men, let us close the argument by repeating that simply to open closed doors to women, admitting them on equal terms to all the usual masculine careers, will not give us equality, for the very simple reason that *the opening of doors is not reciprocal.* In woman's house is a large room the door of which is forever closed to man. The policy of the open door, the "breaking down of sex barriers", leads therefore in practice to a state of society in which women penetrate everywhere under the plea of sex equality, while men are still confined to their traditional fields of work.

It is one of the peculiarities of the feminists that they invariably regard sex barriers as operating against the woman. It has obviously never occurred to a feminist that man also has sex barriers. If men were so foolish as to grumble about the laws of Nature, they might make a grievance out of the fact that they have been debarred for ever from one of the most enriching and unique of all human experiences and opportunities—that of motherhood! Through their sex barrier men are, moreover, cut off from one of the most influential and lucrative of all human occupations—that of wifehood. Consider Tom and his sister Mary. Tom has to work hard to earn his daily bread. No chance for *him* of making a lucky match which will lift him in a trice above all the cares of bread-winning for the rest of his days. But his sister goes to a dance one fine evening and there meets a well-to-do man, who falls in love with her, marries her, and takes her to a nice house where she is waited upon by servants and leads a pleasant life of ease. Tom must still work on, and he is lucky if, at the end of ten or more years of work, he is able to make a home for himself. True enough, there are not, perhaps, very many girls quite so fortunate as the Mary of my illustration. But does anybody deny that they exist? I have myself observed several such cases in the last two or three years. To take a single example: a girl who formerly occupied a very humble position in a small country town that I know attracted the attention of a rich lawyer and is now the mistress of one of the largest houses in the district. Men are not able to leap forward in life in this effortless manner. If the boot were on the other leg, what a fuss there would be in the feminist camp about the masculine monopoly of this short-cut to wealth and ease, and what a shout would go up: "Give us sex equality!"

No man complains because women enjoy this exciting opportunity in life; but they have a right to claim that it should be taken into account in estimating the balance between the sexes. If men possess certain advantages, feminists must not be allowed to forget that women also enjoy some unique privileges.

At this point I must answer a remark ejaculated by the critical reader: "Yes, quite true; but feminists do not want women to have these sex advantages. They wish to give these up, and in exchange to receive true equality. Olive Schreiner, for example, argues eloquently against the parasitic wife or mistress, the woman who 'climbs' by pleasing men!" I know she does. But what difference will this make to the *reality* of the situation? The sex power of women is rooted in our civilisation. Ten thousand feminist writers, be they never so eloquent, cannot abolish it. All

they can do is to express the desire to abolish it. But this
desire will never be fulfilled! The very first step towards
its fulfilment would provoke such a storm of indignation
amongst average women (who are not extreme feminists)
that no further progress could be made with any legislation
in that direction.

Moreover, although most feminists express themselves in
the above sense in their writings, they do not in their practical
political work lay any weight at all on abolishing the
privileges of their sex. They admit in theory that in order to
secure equality women must give up their sex privileges,
but in practice they are not in a hurry to take any steps in
this direction. We shall have to wait a long time before a
woman M.P. will bring in a Bill to render wives equally
liable with their husbands in the eyes of the law. Political
women know well enough that any advance along this line,
in the name of sex equality, would ruin for ever all their
chances of being re-elected to the House.

It is thus very important for the public to draw a distinction between feminist *theory* in all these matters—most of
which is utterly Utopian and impracticable—and feminist
practice. The former urges sex equality. But the latter, by
demanding equality when it would work to the advantage
of women, and not demanding it when it would work to their
disadvantage, tends towards sex privilege rather than sex
equality.

c. The Illusion of Economic Equality

If anyone should still question the purely theoretical
character of the sex equality programme of the Woman's
Movement, let him ponder over *the actual possibilities of this
equality in the world of work*. No matter how sincere our
equalitarians may be in their plea for the removal of sex
barriers, in practice those barriers will continue to stand

which prevent women from undertaking many of the severest and most dangerous types of work, because these are rooted in reality. Even if every occupation were made free to women, such work as coal-mining, sailoring, iron-working, quarrying, and engine-driving would still be carried on almost entirely by men. There is not the slightest danger of any incursions of girl labour in these departments of life. Thus, in practice, supposing the equalitarians had their way, we should get a state of society in which the heavy and dangerous jobs were still performed by the despised male, while women would have established themselves, in at least equal numbers, in all the more pleasant and lucrative lines of work.

I do not make any accusation against feminists, in the sense that they have *deliberately* sought to secure "soft jobs" for their sex. Their desire for equality may be sincere. It is their social philosophy that is inadequate. It is not founded upon an accurate estimate of the respective capacities of men and women, and for this reason leads us from one false position to another.

Seen in the light of reality, the "abolition of sex distinction" is nothing but a hollow catchword. Put into practice, it fails at once, for these distinctions still exist in the world of reality, however much we may seek to banish them from our world of social theory.

The ever-swelling stream of young women who year by year invade the labour market do not act on the principle that there is no sex distinction, nor could they if they would. This stream follows the laws of reality and pours into the lighter types of occupation—secretarial work, commerce, shop-work, bank-clerking—and into the professions. Here it makes itself felt by intensifying competition, and often by undercutting men's wages and salaries. It is hardly possible to say with certainty just how many men have actually been driven into unemployment in this way; but when we reflect that there are some 800,000 women employed in business houses and banks, we obtain some idea of the enormous field of work now occupied by women engaged in doing work which has nothing specifically feminine about it. At the same time, large numbers of competent men (many of whom fought in the war) are looking hopelessly for work.

If sex equality were a reality and not an academic theory, the pressure of female competition in the economic field would be an *equal* pressure. It would distribute itself levelly over the whole area of occupations. Women would then enter such fields of work as mining, railway-work, navvying, and so forth, which are much less desirable from an economic point of view than secretarial and office work. Supposing that of the two million and more women now employed in commerce and industry some million or more were taken up in the heavier kinds of work (as would be the case were they men), this would clearly reduce very considerably their competition in the fields of light and better-paid work. There would at once be a demand for male labour in these fields. The competition of women would then amount, in practice, simply to increasing the number of men in the labour market. As it is, the pressure of female competition is tending to drive men out of the particular types of light and relatively well-paid work which women are able to perform as well as men, and to force men more and more into heavier and lower-grade occupations.

It is not a healthy social condition when a young un-married girl (often living with her parents) earns possibly three pounds a week or more in some form of office or professional work, while an experienced miner or engineer, the father of a family, is lucky if he can get the same. This is a state of things ruinous to the future of the race which permits it. I am not in the least overstating the case when I say that there are tens of thousands of girl typists, secretaries, and business assistants, who spend weekly, on small personal luxuries, more money than many a highly-trained male worker has with which to feed his children. Such conditions are the product of a type of life totally lacking in racial sense (see p. 213).

.   .   .   .   .

In actual life, the equality produced by opening every door to women and "abolishing the barrier of sex" is a complete illusion.

All the doors may be open, but only some of them are entered. Moreover, the door leading to the most spacious chamber in the whole edifice of human work is closed entirely to the male sex. There are more wives dependent upon their husbands than there are workers in any of the various careers and occupations open to men. *The occupation of wifehood is the largest of all the careers open to the young citizen of our country.* And this career is a female monopoly. The complete blind-ness of all feminist writers to this very plain fact is a most curious circumstance, and one for which it is hard to find any explanation. Being a husband is not an occupation by which a man earns his living. But five million women secure their economic existence by being wives (wives earning independently not included). Moreover, wifehood is a career in which the preparation is easy (most often non-existent), and in which the rewards are often very high indeed. There are hundreds of thousands of women in the more well-to-do circles of English society who live all their lives in comfort and ease, doing very little work, sometimes none at all. These women owe their good fortune solely to the fact that they have married a successful man. It would be necessary, in order to establish true sex equality, for men to receive some department of life as a monopoly, just as women possess in wifehood a monopoly calling, since men cannot penetrate equally into feminine fields. Moreover (see p. 131), women have now put forward the demand that their rewards in this main field of female work shall be independent of the work accomplished. If we accept the principle of birth-control (determined by the wife), it means, translated into economic phrase, that a husband must maintain his wife in the style suitable to his position, but that she shall be left free either to fulfil or not to fulfil her wifely functions, just as she may think fit. Now this is a claim that has not been put forward in any male occupation. Therefore, in wifehood, women possess not only an immense field of work, free from all male competition, but an occupation in which they claim to enjoy advantages not enjoyed by men in any masculine occupation—namely, the advantage of themselves determining the amount of work they shall do, or whether they shall do any at all (in as far as maternity, the main branch of the occupation wifehood, is concerned).[1]

To sum up the position: strict equality in the economic field is out of the question. The attempt to create a so-called equality, by securing the admission of women to masculine spheres of work, whilst a vast sphere of feminine work (often light and highly paid) remains barred to men, can only result in a state of things which is unfair to male interests. In Chapter VIII an attempt is made to explain how a more genuine equality might be obtained.

.   .   .   .   .

Moreover, unless we have lost all sense for the deep psychological differences between the sexes, this so-called equality is

[1] It may, of course, be true that, in most marriages, these delicate questions are a matter of mutual agreement, rather than of determination by the wife alone; but this does not affect my point, namely, that the *right* to control birth is claimed by feminists for the wife; she is to have the deciding voice. (See p. 112.)

not really of advantage to women. *The whole idea that this is equality at all is based upon a complete fallacy.* It is assumed that what pleases a boy will be equally pleasing to a girl.

Genuine equality of opportunity can be brought about only by providing for each girl a chance of realising *her* own personality equal to that possessed by the boy of realising *his* own personality. In reality, the number of girls who wish to enter some career or occupation as their final life-aim (without any thought of marriage) is probably very small indeed. If we accept the view that the normal boy wishes to be an engineer or a sailor, and the normal girl wishes to be a mother, it is perfectly clear that to achieve equality of opportunity we must make the possibility of marriage for the girl equal to the professional possibility, in engineering or what not, for the boy. In other words, it is quite idle to set up theories about equality of opportunity which do not take into account the wide difference of outlook between boy and girl, resulting from their different racial tasks. But if we aim in this direction, we must travel along a path quite other than that which has been struck out by the equalitarian feminists, whose programme, as we have seen elsewhere, tends greatly to reduce the marriage opportunity of the modern girl. The kind of equality of opportunity aimed at by the average feminist is one which may be satisfactory to the masculine-minded type of girl, but is wholly illusory to the normally orientated girl who does not find her life fulfilled by being able to enter (say) an engineer's office.

The following illustration will make my point still clearer. Let us suppose that a number of Englishmen and Italians are living on an island in the Pacific, and that the island is governed by the English. In course of time the Italians find life dull, and seeing that the English have made a golf course and a cricket ground, they claim, on the ground of race equality, the right to share in the course and ground. With the idea of giving the Italians the same opportunities, the golf course and cricket pitches might be thrown open to them. Considered superficially, this would seem equality. But in reality it is not! *The typical Italian does not want to play golf or cricket.* He would wish to dance or to play the guitar. If we assume that a certain small minority of Italians happened to be cricketers or golfers, and from the point of view of their own selfish interests led an agitation for so-called racial equality on the island, we should then have an almost complete parallel to the present demand for equality of opportunity between the sexes. The demand for the right of entry of women into every conceivable masculine occupation has been led mostly by women who themselves happen to enjoy this kind of life, just as an occasional Italian may be a golfer, but who do not really represent the deeper and more typical desires of their sex.

d. The Modern Muddle

It is sufficiently obvious to a critical observer that the relationship of the sexes in England and America (and in other Western lands not under Catholic influence) is now in a state of chaos.[1] Modern ideas grow in strength from day to day, yet our law and social practice remain deeply permeated with traditional influences. These influences

[1] "The manners and morals, the laws and arrangements between the sexes to-day, the expectations people have and the rights they claim in love and marriage, constitute now a vast, dangerous, unhappy conflict and confusion. It has ceased to follow a code or a system. It is like a panic, like a *débâcle*. In the past there has been stress, suppression, and sorrow in sexual life, but never so chancy, unjust, and wasteful a time as this one. It is a state of affairs in which no one is safe for happiness and no conduct sure of success. For most of us there is an obligation to blunder. . . ." (H. G. Wells, *The World of William Clissold*, bk. vi, pt. 3.)

continue, by virtue of a kind of inertia, to exert a power long after the life-philosophy upon which they rested has ceased to command general assent.

It is possible to sort out of the muddle certain of the more decisive factors. Perhaps the most important of these is the feudal tradition, which made woman at one and the same time an object of chivalrous consideration and respect and a legal subordinate.

Not a little of the present confusion is traceable to the conflict between this conception of the sex relationship and the much more modern idea of equality. The full depth of this conflict is often very imperfectly realised. A respect for women has become firmly rooted in the mentality of the well-bred man of the Western lands, and in many social matters he is trained from boyhood upwards to give way to women and to treat them with especial deference and consideration. This attitude has been further strengthened through the influence of Puritanism, and reaches its highest manifestation in the New England States of America, where women are in a position of almost complete ascendancy in family and social life. Few thoughtful people will deny that there is a great beauty and value in the idea of chivalry, and that we should lose much of the very best in Anglo-Saxon life if it were to pass away. But it is seldom adequately realised that this conception of woman's social position comes into downright conflict with the idea of sex equality. It is now often assumed that sex equality has won the day. But it cannot really win until the whole tradition of chivalry, and all that it stands for, has vanished completely from our national life. The standing that women enjoy in the United States, at any rate in certain wide social circles, is no doubt one that is highly agreeable to the majority of women (who are not fanatical equalitarians), combining as it does the advantages of equality with the privileges derived from the feudal tradition; but we must be perfectly clear in our minds that this is not sex equality. In modern controversy upon the sex question this point has received far too little emphasis.

There are, speaking roughly, four possible solutions of the problem of woman's social standing:

In the first place, there is *complete* sex equality, involving the abolition of privilege (male or female), and the uprooting from the masculine mind of all special courtesy and consideration towards women. Whether even the ardent feminist would like this society if she ever experienced it is a matter I leave on one side.

In the second place, we have the state of things which I may describe as equality *cum* feminine privilege. This we see in a strongly marked form in America. If further developed, this type of social system tends to become a matriarchy.

Thirdly, we have the downright subordination of women, as witnessed in the East (a solution that does not preclude a very powerful feminine influence in the family).

Fourthly, it is possible to conceive of a sex equality resting upon a system of balance, by which women still received all that men feel is due to their sex, according to the best traditions of Western life (and what the majority of women would probably still prefer to receive); while men, in order to establish equality, would be granted certain privileges roughly balancing the social advantage obtained by women. In an imperfect way the feudal system attempted this, and *at its best* it did really achieve what was (regarded from this point of view) something not unlike sex equality (as admitted, indeed, by Olive Schreiner). It must be remembered that upper-class women at this period enjoyed educational advantages which were in some respects actually superior to those open to their brothers. A grossly exaggerated idea of woman's subordination prior to the Reformation is far too common in present-day feminist literature.

.   .   .   .   .

The modern chaos is best understood when we approach it from a historical standpoint. The sex relation under the feudal system was based upon the allocation of spheres of influence to men and women, the latter being the subordinates of the men, as the men were, in their turn, of their superiors in the mediæval hierarchy. The husband undertook to support his wife and family; while the wife, in her turn, was bound to render feudal service to her husband, in the shape of domestic duties and general obedience. At the same time women, in the higher classes, possessed valuable social privileges.

What has happened to this conception of life in its contact with the modern world is very important. Women have now obtained, in most respects, the same rights as men. At the same time the wife retains the sheltered position which she acquired under the feudal system, together with the accompanying privileges.

The authority and privileges which the husband formerly possessed have disappeared with the coming of sex equality. Not so his duties and burdens. These remain. The man of to-day is bound to maintain his wife and family, to fight for them, to pay taxes for them, and even to bear the penalties for many of their misdemeanours—although in our social practice they are no longer his subordinates.

With women the reverse process has taken place. They have succeeded in converting their traditional duties and burdens from legal obligations into acts of volition, while at the same time retaining their privileges. It is, of course, true that countless women, all up and down the land, are bravely carrying on arduous domestic tasks, just as they did a hundred or more years ago. But the point is that they are not legally bound to do so as they were under the feudal system. In the working classes, of course, far less change is noticeable, for the hard-working life of the average woman in this level of life is conditioned rather by economic necessity than by any masculine tyranny or legal compulsion. It is especially in the upper and middle classes that we see how completely the wife has emancipated herself. In this section of society the husband often works very hard to maintain his wife and family, while no obligation rests upon the wife to do anything at all. Innumerable women of this class spend their whole time golfing, motoring, dancing, and in the social round. (Cf. the articles upon "The Leisured Woman" in *Time and Tide*, in the winter 1926–27.)

At present the utmost confusion and ignorance prevails with regard to all these problems. Very few Englishmen are in the least awake to their own position. We see in the paper, as in a recent case, that the magistrate asks: Has Father any rights? Or a judge writes to the Press explaining that women have gradually become the privileged sex in the eyes of the law.[1] But the general public seems unaware of the revolutionary change that has come about in the position of men in England in the space of less than two generations.

It would appear that the public has been hypnotised by the phrase "sex equality", while being too lazy to analyse the problems presented under this head. In order to establish

[1] Sir Edward Parry, in the *Sunday Chronicle*, February 12, 1928: "Now that woman is legally on her own, it is both degrading to her status as well as unjust that she should maintain the legal privileges which were necessary to her in her chattel days. . . . A husband is still liable for his wife's income-tax and most of her debts, and when she goes trespassing in the next-door garden, or calling her dearest friend next door ugly names, or boxing the ears of her neighbour's little boy, it is the husband who has to pay."

real sex equality it would be necessary to make a clean sweep and start on a fresh basis—a thing which is never done in England.

The present anomalies are due to the fact that the law of the land assumes a feudal family structure which, in modern life, no longer exists. Legally, the man is still head of the family, and only on this assumption is the law just. In reality he has no authority over his family, because in social practice the principle of equality has won the day. In a large number of cases the man himself is a convert to equality and has no desire to play a feudal rôle. Under these conditions it is an absurd anachronism that a man should be held responsible for his wife's debts, and a still greater absurdity that he should be liable for her maintenance if he does not wish to live with her—although she can separate from him at any moment without incurring any financial liabilities.

This curious state of things has resulted from the decomposition of the semi-feudal view of sex relationships when brought into contact with the ferment of new ideas.

Very few of the equalitarians have grasped the immense difficulties that would have to be overcome in order to realise their conception of equality. Only a small band of extremists are prepared to suggest that a man should not be legally responsible for his wife and children. Yet it is idle to talk of equality if men are to be saddled with serious responsibilities from which women are free. But in order to bring about an equalisation of responsibilities in the eyes of the law it would be needful to remodel the whole economic life of the nation, and to endow wifehood and motherhood to an extent that would not be practicable under any social system that we can envisage.

The more deeply we delve into the equality question, the more complications it reveals. The social and domestic aspect of the matter is much more serious than the legal.

We have seen that the feudal system, the influence of which upon English life and law has been, and still is, immense, conferred upon women important privileges, chiefly of the unwritten order, and these have become deeply rooted in English life. Since the emancipation of women has not destroyed these privileges, it has come about that the woman of to-day in any sort of conflict with the other sex, whether public or private, finds herself armed with two weapons. In the one hand she carries her newly won equality, and in the other her social and legal privileges. If the one weapon will not secure victory, she can always use the other. The result of such a conflict is accordingly, in the majority of cases, a foregone conclusion—more especially as the man, either through chivalry or through fear of ridicule, will frequently not employ his legal weapons.

Many feminists are no doubt sincere advocates of equality, and are deficient rather in logic than in sincerity. But there are not a few women who, without sharing the ideals of the genuine feminists, employ their phraseology for their own purposes. Such women are capable of standing upon the principle of equality at one moment, while at another trading upon masculine chivalry to the uttermost.

Let us consider such a case as the following, which is by no means imaginary: A is a young man who has worked hard for some ten years or more to make a position for himself and obtain a home of his own. He has been married for five years to a "modern girl", whose attitude to all the problems of marriage consists in the assertion of her own right to freedom in every circumstance—she will not have any children; she will only do just a little housework, in so far as it amuses her; she insists upon living in a fashion which suits her tastes, but which is contrary to her husband's wishes. The man, however, is expected to work hard and to give up his freedom in every direction. The wife reckons

on her husband's sense of chivalry being always strong enough
to prevent his doing anything actually to coerce her, and she
herself will never go far enough to give ground for divorce.
In this way a regular enslavement of the young husband
has been brought about. In a situation of this kind the wife
appears to hold every trump card in the pack. She is able
to compel her husband to maintain her "in the style to which
she has been accustomed", and to provide her with servants
to do all the housework; while she airily refuses to perform
all the ordinary functions of a married woman. It may be
asked: "Why does not the young husband do something?
Why does he not 'put his foot down'?" But what can he
do? A man cannot take any action against his wife because
she refuses maternity (at any rate not in England, although
there are lands in which it is a ground of divorce). Even if
she went so far as to refuse marital intercourse (a state of
things not uncommon), the husband is practically powerless,
because not one man in a thousand will invoke the law in
matters of this kind (as such women fully realise)—and what
good could it do him if he did?

However much credit such a state of things may be to
the Englishman's chivalry, few people would deny that it
represents a type of married life which is utterly intolerable
from the man's point of view.

It is not very difficult to understand that, given this state
of affairs, the modern man of the educated classes is becoming
less and less willing to put his neck in the yoke. Professor
Wieth-Knudsen tells us, in his studies of Scandinavian
social life, that the result of the feminist modifications of
marriage laws and customs is that divorces are increasing
and marriages decreasing: "by degrees men will decline to
enter the state of matrimony on such conditions".

As we have seen, the whole tangle is due, at bottom, to
the fact that the ideals of freedom and equality have made

infinitely more progress in the mind of the public than they have in the eye of the law. The feudal conceptions which lie at the root of the law have long ceased to exert any moral force in the community. Hobbes said: "The law is the public conscience." Our present difficulties are due to the fact that in these matters the law is wholly out of touch with the public conscience.

.   .   .   .   .

In feminist literature it is the fashion to scoff at the very idea of woman's privileges, as if they were all in the same category as walking on the inside of the pavement— matters of no real significance at all, which would be cheerfully surrendered by women in return for equality. In many cases it seems to be assumed (quite erroneously) that they have already been surrendered. A woman Member of Parliament recently wrote: "Sex privilege is now a thing of the past." Yet when it comes to the point, even the more extreme feminists soon make it clear that they are by no means disposed to abandon their position in matters of privilege. Take one of the very smallest of the Anglo-Saxon woman's privileges—the right to salute or recognise men first in the street or in society. This is a little thing, but it gives women a very considerable advantage in social matters, placing the initiative in their hands, and not, as in Italy or France, in the hands of the man. It is practically a certainty that if this were made a test question, not ten feminists in a hundred (in the cultured classes) would be willing to give up this trifling privilege. The educated Englishwoman is so thoroughly accustomed to enjoy this, and a dozen other social advantages, that she is genuinely unaware of the fact that they are sex privileges, and probably does not in the least realise how hard she would find it to abandon them.

It is hardly necessary for me to draw attention here to other far more important privileges (some of these are referred to on pp. 115 and 120). Women who write of their sex privileges as if they no longer had any weight or value are oblivious of some very important inequalities of marriage law which work to the advantage of the wife. If a husband quarrels with his wife, or becomes unhappy in his home, unless he can get a divorce he must either endure silently or, if he decides to give up living with his wife, pay heavily in maintenance. But the woman who tires of her husband has only to walk out of the house and no one can compel her to return or to pay a farthing.[1]

There are even numerous cases in which women who have deserted their husbands still draw maintenance (although this could not, of course, be enforced by law). So strongly is the feudal sense of responsibility embedded in the mentality of many men of the cultured classes (and not only in these classes), that it is a common occurrence for a husband to "liberate" the wife who no longer desires to live with him and make her a generous allowance. While writing this chapter I saw in the Press mention of a case in which the husband continued to allow his wife a large portion of his handsome income although he knew well that she was living with another man. Thus, in considering both the legal privileges of women and those privileges which depend upon custom or upon the chivalry of particular men, we are made

[1] A legal expert writing recently in the *Evening Standard* said: "A wife can now desert her husband when she likes, and, if there is no other man in the case, return to him or require him to support her. She can do this as often as she pleases, and if he refuses to take her back she technically 'deserts' her. When that happens, she can go to a court and obtain an order compelling him to pay part of his income to her. On the other hand, a husband who has deserted his wife has no right to change his mind—a feminine privilege only—or require her to live with him." The wife can then live apart from the husband while compelling him to support her. It will be seen that a complete equalisation of the law as regards these matters would place women in a far worse position than that which they now occupy.

to realise very forcibly that the wife at present enjoys a position which is altogether superior to anything she could obtain under a system of *strict* sex equality.

The more we thus analyse the implications of strict sex equality, the more it becomes clear that the first steps taken in this direction would be fiercely resisted by nine women out of ten, as soon as they saw their privileges threatened. The enthusiasm of a large body of present-day women for equality is explicable solely by the fact that the name "equality" has been muddle-headedly attached to a state of things which is, in reality, the second solution in our four categories, namely, *equality cum privilege*. It is axiomatic that complete sex equality will never be established in any community in which women possess political power.

A full appreciation of the importance of functional difference will, however, lead us by degrees to another type of equality, of the kind indicated in the fourth of the foregoing solutions, an equality based upon *realities* and aiming at a just balance of opportunity and privilege as between men and women.

e. WOMEN'S RIGHTS AND MEN'S RIGHTS

The situation outlined in the foregoing section may be restated in the following form: the man of to-day is a free individual only in those departments of life in which his conduct is not defined and restricted by the law of the land. If we consider the married man, in particular, we see that his relationship to his wife is regulated in many important respects by an outside authority. But the girl or woman of to-day does not recognise any authority whatsoever. She regards herself as wholly emancipated.

But, it may be asked, must not a woman obey the law of the land as much as any man? This is certainly true. But the important point in this connection is that *woman's chief sphere does not lie under public law.* Traditionally, woman has for this very reason been subordinate to man, while man was subordinate to the State. In the feudal period the State compelled obedience from the husband in respect of maintaining his family, payment of taxes, military service, legal responsibility for his subordinates, and so on. It then fell to the man to see that his subordinates performed their duties properly. He was the representative of the State in the family.

What has happened through the Woman's Emancipation Movement is that woman has emancipated herself from the authority of her former law-giver, *the man* (in her chief sphere, the family); while man cannot emancipate himself from his law-giver, *the State.* It thus comes about that the woman of to-day, even a flapper of eighteen years of age, has more freedom than a man—more than her own father, for example, or her own future husband. The essence of the situation is seen with peculiar clearness when we consider the most elementary duties: the law strictly holds the husband to his primary task of providing for his family, to the point of confiscating his property and imprisoning his person; but the law exercises no control over the wife in point of her primary tasks.

The entire position represents a muddle in which there are no guiding principles. The old ideas have ceased to have any binding force, while the new ideas have not yet evolved any suitable social framework. Our law and social practice have gradually altered under the pressure of events, and we have drifted, without any clear plan, into a quite unforeseen situation.

.   .   .   .   .

After the diligent perusal of a large mass of modern feminist literature, I have not been able to discover that (according to feminist opinion) a husband has any "rights" at all, of any description.

A table of matrimonial rights and duties, as tabulated by the average Anglo-Saxon emancipated woman, would apparently read as follows:

Wife's Rights.—The right of maintenance. The right to work outside the home (even against the wish of her husband). The right to determine the place of her residence. The right to invite her friends to the home and entertain them (at her husband's expense). The right to accept or refuse motherhood. The right (in a certain class) to delegate the housework to servants, who must, of course, be paid by the husband. The right of "complete self-possession" (meaning, presumably, that the modern wife no longer recognises that sex union is a part of the marriage contract). And, in a general sense, the right to full "personal freedom".

Husband's Rights.—None.

Lest the reader might feel inclined to regard this table as a joke, I assure him that I have entirely failed to find a single right which the husband is supposed to enjoy in return for all the concessions which he is expected to yield.

The right of so-called "birth-control", or "free mother-hood", is a main plank in the platform of feminism. And it must mean that the wife has the right to refuse mother-hood, even though the man may strongly desire to have children. At any rate, I feel certain that no feminist would urge that a wife should give way on this point and consent to bear children against her own wish in order to please a man. The right to determine the place of residence has been expressly insisted upon by many leading feminists, and, quite recently, I read an indignant paragraph in an important woman's paper protesting against the notion that a husband should have the deciding word in this matter. Similarly, the right to work outside the home has been specially stressed of recent years by English feminists. Yet if a woman's work in the home be looked upon as balancing the maintenance which she obtains from the husband, it does not seem unreasonable that the husband should have the right to insist that she should at any rate do this work properly and not spend her time elsewhere.

With regard to the main problem, that of maintenance, I have deliberately spoken of the *average* woman of emancipated views. It is true that a small band of more logical feminists demand the economic freedom of married women. But these extremists have never exerted any great influence in England, and the average woman still envisages the husband as the financial supporter of the home. A peculiarity of the situation lies in the fact that the principal spokesmen of the Woman's Movement never commit themselves to any statement of just what the wife is expected to do in return for her maintenance, while their own watchword of complete freedom for women seems to abolish all the traditional duties of wifehood. If a wife is not held bound to sex intercourse, or to maternity, or to household work, it is not clear to what she is bound, if to anything at all! As a matter of fact, feminist writers have not attained to any clarity upon these matters. With the exception of the "out-and-outers" who want to do away with marriage in the interests of freedom (the logical upshot of the cult of complete independence), the leaders of the Movement have been content to preach freedom and put forward a long list of "rights" without seeing at all clearly where this must lead. They have themselves, very probably, not been fully aware of the extent to which the interests of the husband and his point of view have been overlooked. For this reason it is all the more important that a chapter such as the present should be written. My purpose is not in the least to attack modern women, but merely to throw more light upon the real nature and complexity of the problem of equality, with the wish to work towards a just and helpful solution.

It is necessary, further, to remove the impression that these difficult questions should be regarded as made up of "rights" on the one side or the other. In this I merely borrow the method of the feminists. If women may demand right after right, it cannot be wrong for men to ask a mild question or two as to their rights. I realise, of course, that in a fortunate marriage these difficulties do not arise. Where there is true mutual regard and respect people do not stand on their rights. But we cannot overlook the less smooth cases. There must be some definite, recognised system of rights to which appeal can be made. The present chaos is in the long run quite impossible. Its continued existence is a moral and social danger.

In practical life most feminists are, no doubt, more reasonable than would seem probable from their literary utterances, and there are plenty of happily married couples in which the wife, and perhaps the husband too, hold views such as the foregoing. In an ordinary way the happiness of a marriage does not depend upon the abstract views held by the man and woman concerned. The impossibility of the present situation becomes apparent, however, when feminists make their influence felt in the political and social field. It then becomes clear that their attitude towards marriage may be summed up in the phrase: a wife has rights but no duties; a husband has duties but no rights. Mr. Justice Swift recently stated that "no one now suggests that a man can control what his wife does or says". And Lord Merrivale said, on January 18, 1928 (as reported in the Press), that in spite of the equalisation of the sexes, "the changes made have not altered a modern woman's privileges: this is apt to be forgotten."[1] If this is true, and if the law still holds the husband to all his legal obligations, we have a situation in which men are responsible but women are irresponsible. If this state of things becomes established, women will obtain a position in society altogether superior to that of men. The husband will be virtually the slave of his wife. He will be compelled to share his income with her and to work for her, while she will have full control over her own income and person.[2]

[1] Lecturing on "English Law", Professor J. E. G. de Montmorency recently stated that the married woman was "the spoiled darling of the English law". He said that to-day the whirligig of time had brought the revenge that a married woman had more rights than her husband —not only might her civil wrongdoing (even *before* marriage) fall on the husband, but her liability to strangers in contract was limited to her separate estate, while some of her crimes could be imputed to the concern of her husband. (Reported in *The Times* of August 1, 1928.)

[2] It is a sign of the growing reaction against feminism that many of the most thoughtful women are themselves beginning to see that there is really a man's side to the case, and that women cannot eat their cake and have it—claim equality and yet benefit by important privileges. Thus in the *Westminster Gazette* of January 11, 1928, we find Miss Ella Hepworth Dixon saying that whereas bachelors may have a "good time", the modern husband has to accept all sorts of responsibilities quite incompatible with sex equality: "he is not only responsible for his own delinquencies, but for those of his wife as well. The modern husband has no control at all over his wife's doings, yet he is responsible if she libels a friend or piles up debts which she cannot pay, and moreover he is bound to support her for life, however repulsive and bad-tempered she may turn out to be. If she prefers someone else and he is a 'sahib', he is supposed to take all the blame and produce the necessary evidence which will set the ill-assorted couple free. After this chivalrous act the husband has to pay alimony, as well as support the children, whom he is not supposed to be fit to see. In short, the question of Men's Rights requires well airing, and should command the sympathy of the thoughtful of both sexes." It would be a good thing if many of the feminists who rail against the brutality of men, and so forth, were to study some of the recent divorce cases in which the husband has taken upon himself a blame from which he was, in reality, wholly free, solely out of chivalrous consideration for a woman who wished to leave him.

In Mr. Mencken's *In Defence of Women* (see sections 28 and 29) we find an account, in that writer's characteristic style, of the parlous standing of the American husband—a position which is attributed to "the inordinate sentimentality" and "donkeyish vanity" of the modern man (which makes him view the "incapacity of his wife as in some vague way a tribute to his own high mightiness", and desire his wife to be "a sort of empress without portfolio, entirely discharged from every unpleasant labour and responsibility") combined with the "intellectual enterprise and audacity of woman". "No more than a century ago, even by American law, the most sentimental in the world, the husband was the head of the family firm, lordly and autonomous. His sovereignty and dignity were carefully guarded by legislation the product of thousands of years of experience and ratiocination. He was safeguarded in his self-respect by the most elaborate and efficient devices, and they had the support of public opinion. To-day, by the laws of most American States—laws proposed, in most cases, by maudlin and often notoriously extravagant agitators and passed by sentimental orgy—all of the old rights of the husband have been converted into obligations. He no longer has any control over his wife's property; she may devote its income to the family or she may squander that income upon idle follies and he can do nothing. She has equal authority in regulating and disposing of the children, and in the case of infants more than he. There is no law compelling her to do her share of the family labour: she may spend her whole time in cinema theatres or gadding about the shops as she will. She cannot be forced to perpetuate the family name if she does not want to. She cannot be attacked with masculine weapons, e.g. fists and fire-arms, when she makes an assault with feminine weapons, e.g. snuffling, invective, and sabotage. Finally, no lawful penalty

can be visited upon her if she fails absolutely, either deliberately or through mere incapacity, to keep the family
habitat clean, the children in order, and the victuals eatable.
Now view the situation of the husband. The instant he
submits to marriage, the wife obtains a large and inalienable
share in his property, including all he may acquire in
future; in most American States the minimum is one-third,
and, failing children, one-half. He cannot dispose of his
real estate without her consent, he cannot even deprive
her of it by will. She may bring up his children carelessly
and idiotically—and he has no redress. She may neglect
her home, gossip and lounge about all day, put impossible
food upon his table, steal his small change, pry into his
private papers—and he can do nothing. Let him undertake
the slightest rebellion, over and beyond mere rhetorical
protest, and the whole force of the State comes down upon
him. If he corrects her with the bastinado or locks her up,
he is good for six months in jail. If he cuts off her revenues,
he is incarcerated until he makes them good. And if he
seeks surcease in flight, taking the children with him, he
is pursued by the *gendarmerie*, brought back to his duties,
and depicted in the public Press as a scoundrelly kidnapper,
fit only for the knout. In brief, *she* is under no legal necessity
whatsoever to carry out her part of the compact at the
altar of God, whereas *he* faces instant disgrace and punishment for the slightest failure to observe its last letter. The
scene I depict is American, but it will soon extend its
horrors to all Protestant countries. The newly enfranchised
women of every one of them cherish long programmes of
what they call social improvement, and practically the
whole of that improvement is based upon devices for
augmenting their own relative autonomy and power."

The situation so vividly described above is, no doubt,
due, in the main, to the characteristic one-sidedness and

passionate single-mindedness of women. The feminist
leaders are so wrapped up in their affair that they are
simply oblivious of the other side of the case. It is therefore
hardly just to denounce them as mere seekers after power.
Moreover, the belief of many feminists that women will
use their power in order to purify and elevate our civilisation is so sincere that we cannot fairly accuse them of vulgar
self-interest, however much we may differ from them.[1]

But the true feminist idealists should be on their guard
against allowing their movement to degenerate into such
a pursuit of power. They must make up their minds whether
they want sex equality or whether they want to increase the
privileges of women. Both these paths cannot be pursued
at the same time. The genuine advocates of sex equality
should be the first to denounce the conditions to which
Mr. Mencken refers, since they make a mockery of the
idea of equality. Unfortunately, but very naturally, the
women who are inspired with a high ideal of equality are

[1] The view held by Professor Eberhard (*Feminismus und Kulturuntergang*), that we have to deal with what is definitely an Amazonian movement, a deliberate attempt to seize for women the leadership in the
State and drive men down to a lower social level, is no doubt greatly
exaggerated. The present work is written from quite another standpoint.
But there is, possibly, rather more truth in his view-point than would
be admitted by feminists themselves. It would certainly seem to be
the case that the idea of sex equality does not play the same part in the
Woman's Movement that it did twenty or thirty years ago. The battle
then raged around the levelling down of sex distinction, while now it
turns more upon the attempt to secure for women every possible advantage. This is especially obvious in America, where the idea of equality
has quite sunk into the background. In Russia, too, there is practically
nothing left of sex equality in the laws (passed under feminist influence)
concerning marriage, divorce, and maintenance. According to Eberhard, the love of power (especially power over persons) is much stronger
in women than it is in men; and accordingly the danger of women
exerting their political influence to enforce all sorts of tyrannical legislation—a kind of extension of nursery government into politics—is to be
taken very seriously.

a small minority when compared with those who regard the Movement as a means of improving the position of women in every possible way and securing for them the maximum of sex privilege, as well as the removal of existing inequalities where these favour men. This is unquestionably the danger-point of the present crisis. It would be possible to move forward to a better social system, a true co-operation between men and women. But it is also possible to follow the American example and drift, without perceiving clearly where we are going, into a kind of muddle of degenerate chivalry and spurious equality. The chivalry is degenerate because it is not founded upon sound biology and psychology; and the equality is spurious because it does not demand from women the same responsibilities that are placed upon men. True chivalry protects women while demanding from them the competent discharge of their racial functions. The caricature of chivalry to be seen in the modern world reduces the wife to the level of a sexual parasite.

The signs of the times indicate that we are far more likely to move in the second of these two directions than in the first. Even in Germany, a country less liable to such a development than America or England, there is a loud complaint of the ever-increasing decay of home-life and the growth in numbers of the parasitic non-maternal type of woman. Thus Frau Sturmfels writes: "By reason of their too high demands, women in all social classes are making slaves of their menfolk. Husbands are becoming beasts of burden, occupied in producing the wealth necessary for the comfort of their wives, who are themselves too lazy and inefficient to discharge their domestic duties. This Americanism, which makes of the woman a spoiled tyrant in her relationship to home and husband, is seen in its most unendurable form in the well-to-do circles; but it is spreading in the middle class." (Quoted from Eberhard,

Feminismus.) Another German lady, Frau K. von Rosen, declares that the husband of to-day is sinking into slavery; while a third, Frau Laura Marholm, writes: "The majority of women of the higher classes, in the large cities, are hard-hearted parasites." And Frau Grete Meisel-Hess, one of the leaders of German feminism, expresses herself in the same sense.[1]

We all know, it is true, that leading feminists denounce these evils. But the remedies they propose are wholly useless. We thus have a paradoxical situation, in which the Woman's Movement, while itself attacking the above type of woman, is at the same time largely responsible for her existence. It was mainly the influence of feminism which gave rise in America to the one-sided marriage legislation which has so enormously increased the power of the wife over the husband. The whole propaganda of modern feminism, with its repudiation of domestic ideals, has been grist to the mill of the parasitic type of woman, who in former ages was held to definite household duties even while she sought to "climb" by means of her sex attraction, but who now misuses the "rights" which were hardly won for quite a different type of woman and quite another purpose.

The feminist panacea for the trouble is to give the leisured

[1] Mr. R. E. Corder, the well-known police court correspondent of the *Daily Mail*, wrote in the *Sunday Dispatch* of August 5, 1928: "No matter how much a wife may nag, torment, and neglect her husband, he has no redress; but if in a fit of temper he turns upon her, she rushes to the police courts and obtains a separation order, and for *the rest of his life* that husband has to contribute to the support of his wife, who is at liberty to lead any kind of life she pleases. A bad husband may be, and often is, a good investment. Young girls marry, not for a home, but for alimony. Scores and scores of times I have seen in the courts girl wives obtain separation orders from their husbands after a few months of married life. Later I have seen these same girls, well fed, smartly dressed, obtaining summonses for maintenance arrears " (my italics).

dependent wives work outside the home. But they would not take it! This type of woman will never abandon her life of ease and luxury. She knows that she is firmly entrenched behind the barricade of rights won by her sisters of a sterner stamp. The position of personal freedom achieved by the higher class English woman has made her independent of her husband. Many of these women possess either private means or an income settled upon them by their husbands on marriage, so that they are immovably fortified against any attempt on the part of the husband to control them in any way. In a recent case it transpired that the wife had demanded before marriage that the husband should settle upon her, without any conditions, two-thirds of his income, whatever that income might be. There are certainly not many women who would have the "nerve" to suggest an arrangement going so far as this; but it is obvious that all settlements of this kind, if they are entirely unaccompanied by conditions, place the wife in a superior position as compared with the husband. Modern civilisation has thus followed the path of ancient Rome, and brought into existence a considerable class of women who combine wealth and power with complete irresponsibility.

The feminist reader will scoff at the term "conditions". What! The free woman of to-day subscribe to conditions, pledge herself towards her husband—never! And many husbands, with the inborn chivalry of the Western European man, will scorn the suggestion that anything of the kind is needful. *And yet the man always accepts binding conditions when he marries.* No one dreams of regarding this as degrading. Thus we see how far we have drifted away from the idea of sex equality. It now appears almost as a matter of course that the wife should receive a greater degree of freedom than that granted to (or even desired by) the husband.

But even if the idea of careers for wives of the educated

classes were to gain much more ground than is at all likely, it would still be totally impracticable, for the reason that all these women could not find work. The higher walks of life are now crowded to suffocation.

As we have already seen, the drastic remedy for the situation, the repeal of the laws of maintenance, is quite out of the question. The majority of the supporters of the Woman's Movement would revolt at the first suggestion of a move in this direction. Moreover, such a step would not be fair to the great body of wives who are not in sympathy with parasitism, and who are honestly doing their duty to their homes and children. It would leave them at the mercy of their husbands in a far worse sense than was the case with women a hundred years ago.

If the demand for *strict* sex equality ever became widespread (which is highly improbable), it would be needful to undertake a complete revision of our marriage laws (with regard to maintenance, desertion, divorce, etc.) in a sense which would prove very unacceptable to the mass of women (who are not strict equalitarians), since these laws are for the most part framed in the interests of the wife, as the supposed weaker partner.[1]

[1] Nor would this revision stop at the marriage laws. In spite of the conviction of feminists to the contrary, there are a good many laws which strongly favour female offenders. Miss Helena Normanton (the lady barrister) writes of the Criminal Law Amendment Act: "It overloads the scales of justice very heavily against young men, and seems to assume that all young women are sinned against and never sinning." She also remarks that the presence of women jurors is useful in this type of case, because their eyes are not befogged by sentiment in dealing with the "young minx" type of female who comes into court. With an all-men jury the girl has a much better chance (a very interesting little bit of psychology). The main idea of the laws dealing with sex offences is to protect women and girls against men; if these laws were to be drawn up on the basis of strict equality as between the sexes, they would have to be revised in a sense which would not be agreeable to many sections of feminist opinion. As is well known, the bias of such

Equality might be brought about either through throwing the burdens of home-life upon husband and wife alike, or laws (in America especially) is outrageously anti-masculine. About a year ago two young soldiers, slightly the worse for drink, attached themselves to two girls in the street at Omaha and began to molest them, without, however, doing them any harm whatever. They were arrested, brought to the police-station, tried, and sentenced to over ten years' imprisonment each! It is true that this fantastic sentence was commuted to about one year's detention by another court, but as an evidence of the absurdly anti-masculine bias of American justice the matter is worth mentioning. If two girls had begun to fool about with a couple of young men, in nine cases out of ten nothing would have taken place at all, and in the tenth case they might have been fined a dollar or two.

Even in Germany, a country not under feminist influence, the laws are surprisingly partial to the female offender in cases involving assault. Thus a man who kissed a little girl of eight on the knee was recently sentenced to imprisonment; while servant-girls and others who had committed very serious offences against young boys were not punished with any severity. (For numerous examples, see Eberhard's *Feminismus.*) In Austria, adult women found guilty of seducing boys under fourteen years have again and again been set free, while men are most severely punished for similar offences.

Havelock Ellis has drawn attention to the frequency of sexual offences on the part of nurses and servants towards little boys, but it is only in the rarest cases that any punishment results—in the vast majority of cases the parents do not know what has gone on. Dr. Gibb (New York) has borne witness to the comparative frequency of sexual violations in which the girl is the active partner, and to the fact that such cases are seldom punished.

Further, there arises the question of penal measures. Do the feminists wish to see these equalised as between the sexes? And if not, why not? At present flogging is the penalty to which men are exposed for some offences, and several important women's organisations were in favour of this measure at the time when it was under discussion, although women guilty of the same offences were to be exempt from the penalty. If it be alleged that the physical and mental nature of women makes it undesirable to inflict corporal punishment upon female prisoners, I have nothing to say against the argument; but on other occasions these same organisations deny entirely that there are any significant psychological distinctions as between men and women. A somewhat different aspect of this matter is the sentimental bias of courts of justice in favour of female prisoners, especially notorious in the Latin lands and in America. It often reaches such a point that women, simply because through dissolving the home altogether (as a legal institution). If we should follow the first path, the wife would have to be made legally responsible for the upkeep of the home and care of the children to the extent of "fifty-fifty"; if the education of the children cost, say, £1,000, then half of this sum would come from the wife's pocket and the other half from the husband's; and similarly the costs of the household would have to be shared between the man and woman. The second path would lead us to a society in which men and women were free of legal ties, as far as marriage was concerned, and in which the care and education of the children were thrown wholly upon the State or community.

It is clear that neither of these paths can be pursued under existing conditions of life. Even in Russia, after a revolution which shook the world, it was not found practicable to establish equality along these lines, although it was one of the aims of the revolution (as stated, for example, by Trotsky). As we have seen, it is purely impracticable to provide each wife with an income approximately equal to that of her husband; nor is it feasible to throw upon the State the burden of providing for the whole child-life of the community. We are thus left with the conclusion that full equality, as envisaged (at any rate in theory) by the feminists, is a will-o'-the-wisp. But this does not close the door to a moral equality based upon functional differentiation—of which more anon.

  ·   ·   ·   ·   ·

The modern world, and especially the Anglo-Saxon section of it, is managed by people who are "practical"; they are women, and for no other reason, are acquitted of serious crimes (even murder) to which they have pleaded guilty. I witnessed a case in Italy where a girl who had murdered her baby under the most revolting circumstances was acquitted—and subsequently married the prosecuting counsel!

in other words, by those who hate thinking and do not mind where they go as long as they feel they are "progressing". Faced with an alternative, the "practical" politician invariably tries to find a compromise. If he is called upon to decide whether he will spend his holiday at Brighton or Scarborough, his only notion of solving the difficulty is to proceed to Southend, because that is neither north nor south. But sooner or later realities make themselves felt, and it becomes clear that either Brighton or Scarborough would have been far nicer than Southend. And it will not be long before the appalling muddle of our domestic and sex life will convince us that the attempt to solve great problems of life by a series of petty compromises, while steadily refusing to face fundamentals, has landed us in a dead-lock.

In reality, it is as clear as daylight that the principle of individual freedom—the only constant idea in the Woman's Movement—is fundamentally incompatible with monogamous marriage as a legal institution. The principle of self-determination, if applied really logically, annihilates the home as a social unit. Marriage rests upon the idea of union. It calls upon two personalities to surrender their ego-centricity in the interests of a higher entity—the family. But self-determination denies that there is any entity higher than the individual and his self-will. It is this essential antithesis between the individual and the race (represented by the family) which forms the core of the problem Woman and Society. Once grant the principle of freedom, interpreted in a purely individualistic sense, and there is an end of the family. It is the persistent failure of the leaders of the Woman's Movement to face this antithesis and see its depth and significance that has led to the continuously smouldering conflict in the Movement between those who defend monogamy and those who champion free-love, the companionate marriage, and other rivals to the Christian view of the family. This conflict will not so easily be solved by any facile compromise. In the meantime the Movement as a whole continues to follow the path of self-determination. (See Chapter VIII, Section d.)

It is not easy to forecast the future. The signs of the times indicate that the freedom propaganda will make headway, in which case we shall see a gradual disintegration of the family (upon a monogamous basis). Things will move in the direction they have already taken in wide circles of American life—easy divorce, trial unions, companionate marriages, and so on. On the other hand, it is not impossible that the innate conservatism of the British people will assert itself once more, and a serious attempt will be made to tighten up the bonds of marriage. But, taking a wide view of the situation, it would appear that the institution of monogamy is bound up with the tradition of Christianity, and that where the people break away from this religious view of life it will, in practice, be impossible to maintain the Christian family. In the long run people cannot be compelled by laws to support an institution in which they no longer really believe.

A writer on social questions has recently made an interesting suggestion, namely, that *two forms of marriage should be legalised*: one for those who wish definitely to stand upon the traditional ground, and the other for those who believe in the principle of freedom. In the former case the husband would undertake the traditional obligations with regard to maintenance, etc.; while the wife would, on her side, be pledged to accept the usual wifely duties and responsibilities. In the free marriage there would be no pledge on the wife's side; and, on the other hand, the husband would not be legally compelled to support his wife and family—although, in practice, he might do so.

The conditions of divorce might well be different in the two cases. This would perhaps be the best way of meeting the fact that our population is now wholly divided in its outlook on these matters. It would, at any rate, be better than putting our heads in the sand and pretending that nothing has changed!

f. THE NEW MATRIARCHY

During the last twenty years and more a tremendous agitation for the freedom of women and for the improvement of their position in every way has been in progress. Throughout this period men have remained almost wholly passive. The aggressive rôle has been taken over exclusively by the so-called passive sex.

There should be no war between the sexes, destined as they are to assist one another, but it would be futile to deny that, in the modern world, there *is* a conflict, due to the absence of any principle of regulation by which sex interests (which must, in the nature of things, sometimes be opposed) can be balanced. Many feminists seem to take the naïve view that "equality" will have been achieved when women have got everything they want. This comes to light, in an amusing fashion, in the writings of many American women, who put forward, at one and the same time, the view that woman is equal to man, and the claim that woman, as the mother of the race, should receive the status of a semi-divine being, entitled to receive chivalrous consideration from man on every possible occasion—whether she has actually borne any children or not! I should be the last person to say anything against chivalry, but a man may be permitted to point out that the demand that men should give way to women in all matters concerning sex relations and family life (as advanced by these Americans) cannot be brought into line with the idea of sex equality!

In the absence of any regulating principle, it is clear
that the relationship of the sexes must depend chiefly on the
interplay of forces. When men exerted their masculine
authority with vigour, they forced women into an inferior
position. The laws of chivalry developed under the feudal
system were largely an attempt to save women from being
exposed to this free-play of force, by giving them a definite
status and defined privileges. This system has now broken
down. The relation of the sexes is undefined. Now, however,
it is the women who assert themselves. For the last generation or so women have pushed energetically in every direction, while men have not pushed at all. The women's army
has advanced from one captured position to another. The
granting of one demand is immediately followed by the
formulation of new demands, which in their turn are
speedily granted. It is a peculiarity of the feminist mentality
to believe that every advantage won by women must
necessarily be a "right", something of which they have
been wrongfully deprived by oppressive man—although
not a few of their demands, as we have seen, are quite
incompatible with sex equality.

In the absence of all masculine resistance, it would seem
that women might thus gradually advance from one position
to another until the major share of power in the State
rested in their hands. (In this connection it must not be
forgotten that women voters already largely outnumber
men voters.)

A mere advance on the part of women, unbalanced by
any consideration for male interests, will not of itself give
us sex equality. Imagine the situation reversed. Would a
continual advance on the part of men lead *of itself* to a state
of just balance between the sexes? I am sure no feminist
would think that it would. But since, according to the
feminists, women do not differ in their moral characteristics

from men, it must follow that women, too, if left to demand all that they want, might go a long way beyond their just claims. The love of power is certainly not less strong in women than in men.

A state of true sex equality might come about through the arbitrament of some authoritative body, such as State or Church; or it might come about through the balance of power between conflicting forces. But there is no reason to believe that it will come about by way of granting to women everything that they ask. The main purpose of this chapter is to explore the problem of sex equality with a view to preparing the way for such a true equality. It is needful to throw fresh light on the problem, and especially to expose the fallacy of equality of the kind now popularly advocated.

.   .   .   .   .

"None of us can move anywhere without finding that men are trembling before coming events."—Lady Frances Balfour at the National Council of Women at York (October 16, 1928).

For a moment let us make a picture of society as it would be were the demands of the feminists to be fulfilled.

In the first place we should have sex equality in the higher walks of life. Women would share with men all the more lucrative and influential occupations, such as the law, medicine, politics, business, and so on; while as clerks, typists, secretaries, shop assistants, Civil Servants, etc., women would tend to drive men out of the field.

In the second place, nearly all heavy and dangerous work would still be performed by men. In our mines, quarries, ships, and iron foundries men alone would still be employed. While in case of war it would still be men who would have to defend the country.

I

In the third place, women would retain, and even increase, the immense power they wield in the home and in married life. In the home the wife would be a free personality. Not so the husband, who would still be compelled to support his family, and would be pursued by the law if he failed to come up to the mark. Moreover, the unique influence which women exert through being the mothers of the race would be, so to speak, "thrown in".

In the fourth place, women would, of course, continue to wield the power which they possess by virtue of their sex charm and all that attaches to it—a power which is as important and far-reaching as it is elusive of exact definition.

Such a state of affairs would amount, in practice, to *a modern matriarchy*. The idea of sex equality would have been abandoned by the wayside long before this goal was reached. It is interesting solely as a picture of what society might become if it were moulded entirely from the standpoint of women's wishes, without any reasoned attempt to strike a fair balance between the interests of the sexes.

Since feminists would wish greatly to increase the number of women earning their living, and since it is not possible for women to take up the heavier jobs of the kind referred to above, it is clear that an immense flood of women workers would be poured into all the lighter fields of occupation, and this would exert such a tremendous economic pressure that men would be driven out of these fields (as they have already been largely driven out of typing and elementary school teaching). But where would these men find work? Not many of them would be fitted for the professions (in which there would, moreover, be even less room than at present, crowded as they would be with women), and in consequence they would be driven downwards into the harder and lower-paid forms of occupation. They would share the fate of the Italians and Poles in the United States.

They would be good enough to do all the heaviest and worst-paid work; or they would join the unemployed.

When a writer like Olive Schreiner exclaimed dramatically that modern women wish to stand side by side with their men in the battlefields of the world's work, as they did of yore in the forests of the North, when the Romans fought against the Teutonic tribes, she was simply being carried away by her gift for rhetoric. In sober reality it is quite impossible for the normal woman to work as a sailor, an iron-puddler, a quarryman, or a navvy. Further, in *Woman and Labour* there is not a word about the entry of women into these prosaic occupations, all the enthusiasm of the authoress being reserved for work of a more interesting and intellectual type. It may be true that it is by necessity and not by choice that women would tend to monopolise the fields of light work. But this does not affect the situation. It merely shows how completely illusory is the idea of sex equality in the world's work.

.   .   .   .   .

It will no doubt be hastily objected by the reader of feminist sympathies that, even granted the fact that men would continue to perform the severest types of work, *this would be balanced by the risks run by women as mothers of the race.*

This is a most important point. There is truth in this argument in the case of those mothers who bring up large families, since they undoubtedly bear a heavy burden. But is not the advocacy of birth-control, with its elimination of the "unwanted child", part of the platform of feminism? In other words, according to the feminists, women should not be expected to bear children except as a matter of personal inclination. They entirely repudiate the idea of maternity as a duty, and pour scorn on the man who would force a woman to maternity against her wish. This question cannot be discussed here; but it is obvious that those who hold this standpoint cannot, by any possibility, represent the maternal function as an onerous and unpleasant occupation, worthy of comparison with iron-puddling or coal-mining, since, by their own confession, women (in the feminist society) are not to bear children *at all* save for their own pleasure. I do not suppose a coal-miner would regard coal-mining as a hardship if he were free to go down the pit or not, just as he felt inclined, while drawing his wages in any case.

Many readers will no doubt shrink from such a matter-of-fact comparison between coal-mining and maternity. They will argue that the production of a human child is something so sacred, so fraught with significance and potential of tragedy, that maternity cannot properly be compared with any ordinary occupation, such as mining or sailoring (even if these, too, are full of danger). This may be quite true. I have nothing to say against the sacredness of maternity. But I am here purposely placing myself on the feminist ground. It is part of their case that there *is* no essential difference between male and female occupations, and that they *can* properly be compared. And I have proceeded to compare them quite cold-bloodedly. The reader who feels instinctively that there is a vital difference between maternity and any male occupation has thereby admitted that woman's place in society is unique, and that it cannot properly be put on a level with man's place. He has already deserted the ground of sex equality[1] and joined those who think (with me) that society must recognise the essential difference of function between man and woman.

[1] The term "sex equality" is here employed in the sense of the popular catchword, and without prejudice to moral sex equality (on a functional basis).

It is the feminists who say that women do not claim any special consideration on account of sex.

It would be a hopeless task to seek for any definite principle or logic in the utterances of feminists with respect to maternity. Many cannot go far enough in exaltation of the mother and in raptures over the joys of motherhood. Others seek to represent motherhood as a painful and dangerous task analogous to man's service as a soldier in war-time. Very often both points of view are put forward by the same individual.[1] In reality, motherhood is a natural biological function, accompanied by both pain and joy. As such it cannot be compared with soldiering, sailoring, or any other male occupation. The normal woman desires to have children, and is willing to take the risks. But it could not be said of the normal man that he desired to stand for weeks and months in a muddy trench, and was willing to run the risk of being shot in order that he might enjoy this privilege. As Frau Johanna Elberskirchen, a German feminist writer, puts it: It is in woman's own interest to have children; the bearing and feeding of the children

[1] In *Woman and Labour* (p. 169) we find that maternity is represented as a painful sacrifice, "acute anguish and weariness", and a "long, patiently endured strain"; but on page 127 the authoress speaks of maternity as "the crowning beatitude of woman's existence", and expresses the opinion that its joys are full compensation for the suffering involved. In the first case it is sought to show that if men suffer in war, women suffer far more in maternity; whereas on page 127, the end of the argument is to prove that women who are deprived of motherhood suffer a cruel loss. There is, of course, some truth in both points of view; but if the latter line of argument is true, and women do really derive more joy than pain from maternity, it is scarcely possible to make use of maternity as an offset to the sufferings of the soldier. The statement on page 170 (that far more women die in childbed than men in warfare) was written before the Great War, when the number of men killed in four years exceeded many times the number of women who die in maternity in a *century* (taking the figures for Great Britain in each case). Further, the number of men who are killed in industry annually is much larger than the number of women dying in childbirth.

give her acute pleasure (once the actual birth is over), just as every physiological process is pleasurable to the healthy person. "Woman experiences, in the care of her young children, sensations of pleasure which are for ever barred to the man." If there is any truth in this point of view—and who can doubt it?—it is the merest nonsense to compare the function of the willing mother with the monotonous drudgery of the coal-miner or iron-puddler. A woman yearns to have children; but a man does not yearn to stay below the earth in a dark gallery for eight hours a day!

It is just here, in the matter of maternity and birth-control, that we see quite unmistakably that feminism is drifting towards the matriarchal ideal and away from the equality ideal. This is no doubt, in the main, a trend for which the leaders are not *consciously* responsible. Their determination to claim for women conditions of life in which they shall enjoy the fullest possible freedom, has led them, by slow degrees, into a position such that they are now virtually demanding for women a social status altogether different from that occupied by men, and essentially one of sex privilege. Strict equality would demand that if men are compelled to work at their dangerous trades (say coal-mining or iron-puddling) that they may live, women, too, should be compelled to perform their most dangerous occupation (maternity) in order that they may live.[1] The

[1] At this point some reader will say: "Yes, but the endowment of motherhood will solve the problem. Then women will be paid in proportion as they produce children, thus placing them on a level with 'piece-workers'." This may sound very well; but in practice the endowment of motherhood does not mean that women actually *live* by maternity, in the sense that they are compelled to produce children in order to keep the wolf from the door, as the miner is compelled to go down the pit. It means merely that the State covers the cost, or rather a part of the cost, of the child, once the child is born. The wife derives her means of support elsewhere. Moreover, in the middle and upper classes the idea of maternity endowment is impracticable. It is impossible

nation cannot exist without coal or iron; but neither can it exist without children. If it is necessary, in the national interest, that men should be forced down the mines or into the ironworks, it is necessary for the same reason that women should give birth to an adequate supply of children. But the feminists, false to their theories of equality, insist upon making maternal service entirely voluntary, thus giving women a status of privilege, if we look at these problems logically from the standpoint of equality and uninfluenced by sentiment.

It is, of course, *impossible to apply strict equality in these matters*, and so far the feminists are right. Where they are wrong is in the attempt to give currency to their ideals under the name of sex equality, when what they are really doing is to seek to add another to the existing privileges of their sex. I have nothing to say against the enjoyment by women of certain privileges, so long as we all perceive the situation to be what it really is, and if we are willing, in order to balance things, for men to have some rights not possessed by women. Thus a more genuine equality may come into being. But we must not allow ourselves to be led astray by the suggestion that every right granted to women is merely a further step towards sex equality.

g. TOWARDS SEX EQUALITY

Should the foregoing, then, lead us to the conclusion that women in general, or the feminists in particular, are to blame for the present chaotic conditions? Most emphatically not. Nobody could be so foolish as to blame women for

for the State to pay some thousand pounds or more to a middle-class mother in order to recompense her for the expenses of a child. The belief that maternity can be paid by the State and thus placed on an economic level with men's paid work is pure illusion.

seeking to better their social standing and enlarge their opportunities. If the feminist propaganda is one-sided, so is every other political and social movement. And if feminism, in the pursuit of rights, has encroached overmuch upon male territory, it is men themselves who are to blame for their astonishing indifference to matters so closely concerning their vital interests.

There is a deep truth in a remark of Mr. Ludovici's, that "Feminism constitutes a tacit or avowed condemnation of the male population of the country in which it flourishes". It is beyond all question the fact that it is the incapacity of the modern "Western" man to provide inspiring social ideals and an effective organisation of life that has reacted upon the womenfolk of the community. With perfect justice they say: "Look what a mess our men have made of things! Isn't it time we tried our hands?" Those who attend feminist gatherings must have heard this sentiment scores of times. Many women must have felt, too, often unconsciously, that the ghastly tragedy of the Great War constituted an exposure of the man-made social system of the last century. Man, as the sex most endowed with initiative and organisatory power, has conspicuously failed to fulfil those functions expected of him in this respect (that man is by nature better endowed, in this sense, is a fact, in spite of his failure in recent times —in history man has proved again and again that he possesses immense powers of social organisation). The modern woman's cult of freedom and independence does not prove that she really finds her joy in these things. On the contrary, if the right men are there, she prefers to be led; but she will not be led by men who are patently deficient in the quality of leadership. To-day we see the evidences of this bankruptcy of leadership on every hand. In the unemployment mess, in the failure to solve the peace problem, in the industrial crisis (largely due to the lack of foresight of our statesmen), and, not least, in the sex muddle, there is abundant evidence of the complete incapacity of the modern "Western" man to master his social and economic problems in an efficient and purposeful fashion.

No one who has made any study of present-day life and literature could doubt for a moment that *the modern woman's profound dissatisfaction with the man of to-day* is an outstanding feature of the situation. As Storm Jameson, A. M. Ludovici, Oskar Schmitz, and other writers on sex questions have often said, this dissatisfaction plays a far more prominent part than is realised by the majority of feminists themselves. Under modern conditions, we could scarcely look for any other result. It is obvious enough that the more the sexes are educated for one another the more they will please each other. But this is not the goal of education, either male or female, to-day. The modern girl is trained, not to be man's partner but to be an independent creature; the man in his turn (foolishly perhaps) plays up to this attitude and freely grants independence to the women who are connected with or "dependent" upon him. But woman's deepest self does not crave for independence; with her constitution and heredity this would be impossible. She craves for self-fulfilment along the lines of her own inherent qualities. In helping her to independence (but *not* to self-fulfilment along feminine lines) the man of to-day is bringing to expression in the woman the masculine side of her character (which ought to be in recession); in consequence, her female instincts are starved and she resents the stupidity of the male, who through his own lack of masculinity (towards her) has put her in this position. If all that woman wants is independence, then why does she marry at all? If she does marry, it is clear that she must be looking, not for independence but for something quite different. Does the man of to-day supply this other want? In reality, there is and *must be* a *fundamental antithesis* between the impulse towards *union* which impels a woman to marry and the acquired ideal of complete independence (the ideal of perfect *dis-union*). It is the presence in her mind of this unsolved problem which wrecks her happiness. One part of her personality cries out for independence (her High-School soul, as Mr. Ludovici would say), but another and more ancient part craves for fulfilment through the male, in other words for dependence. But if the male is to answer this need, he must be a real male, and not a mere boyish comrade who carries into marriage the spirit of the golf-course. There is an age for *camaraderie*, and there is an age for deeper things, for the new responsibilities born of adult life. The school prepares the girl (and for that matter the boy, too) for this first stage, but not for the second. The reason for this is that the school has no real philosophy of life behind it.

We come back to the basic fact that to-day neither sex is properly adjusted to the *other*. The true psychological contacts are no longer sought. In the sphere of sex there is a complete failure to face fundamentals.

.   .   .   .   .

A most trenchant and penetrating treatment of this side of our problem is to be found in *Woman: A Vindication*, where Mr. Ludovici, after explaining that women are, in their inmost natures, *the custodians of the race*, says: "The voice of Life inside them tells them emphatically that things are wrong, that the muddle man has made of Life is tragic, cruel, insufferable." The revolt of women, he then explains, is essentially a symptom to which we ought to pay the most careful attention. It is the voice of a being nearer to Nature than is the male, more primitive, and therefore more keenly aware of what is unnatural. It is the profound discontent of women with the one-sided, rationalistic, over-intellectual, mechanised and de-spiritualised civilisation of to-day that has stung her to bitterness and fierce protest. He continues, "As woman is immersed in Life, she has not the duality of vision that is necessary for placing and ordering Life". As the mother of the race, she feels in her bones when things are going wrong, when the future life of her children is being endangered by bad conditions of life or false social ideals; and she is accordingly resentful towards the men who have so bungled their job. But she feels this without herself being possessed of the more masculine qualities of synthesis and organisation needful to save the situation.

The startling decline of the birth-rate amongst the more intelligent classes is largely due to the feeling (sometimes unconscious) of the women of these classes that life has ceased to have any profound purpose for which it is worth while to make the effort to continue the race. I have often heard women say: "Why should we bring children into the world to be destroyed in another war?" Others say: "Why should we struggle to rear families, when all that confronts them is a life of meaningless drudgery in the factory or office?"

As we shall see in the following chapter, it is, with the very rarest exceptions, men who originate our great ideals and provide our spiritual inspiration (all the founders of religions have been men!). And it is, therefore, men who are firstly responsible for the materialism of modern life. The revolt of women, whether vocal or not, whether it takes the form of agitation or the form of refusing to continue the race, is at bottom a negation of life, as life is at present constituted.

But is not this a justification of feminism? a reader may

ask. It is a justification of true feminism, based upon a full recognition of sex difference. But it in no way supports typical equalitarian feminism. If men have made a mess of things, it is obvious that women can help to find a way out only in so far as they are different from men. The education of women along masculine lines and their absorption in male occupations will merely infect women with the prevailing masculine mentality, which, as we have seen, is totally ineffective. It is, above all things, needful that woman should be true to herself if she is to supplement man. The more men have muddled things, the more important it must be that women, at any rate, should retain some positive principle of life uncorrupted by male degeneration. The inability of the feminist of to-day to perceive this very obvious connection is one of the most curious features of the crisis. It would almost seem as if the more feminists despised men and criticised their social incapacity, the more determined they became to imitate them in every way!

While the world never needed the positive and characteristic woman more than it does to-day, it is clear, for reasons already explained in the foregoing sections, that the Feminist Movement of to-day would need an entirely fresh orientation before it could be of the slightest use in clearing up the muddle. It is not a case of men *or* women, but men *and* women. We need the kind of co-operation between the two which can only be worked out upon the basis of a frank recognition of their essential difference and interdependence. The evolution of a pseudo-masculine type of woman, who may lose her own specific womanliness, but will certainly not acquire the best masculine qualities, can only serve to make confusion worse confounded.

The key to the situation lies in an accurate understanding of the psychology and social functions of man and woman. And accordingly this chapter will now conclude, in order that we may proceed to a discussion of the more important differences between the sexes.

.   .   .   .   .

The present confusion is characteristic of an age of transition (it could best be compared to the conditions in the latter-day Roman Empire).

Not for a moment is it suggested that—even were such a development conceivable—women should be put back into any position of inferiority. But it is essential to throw a sharp light upon the impracticability of doctrinaire sex equality, thus better to clear the way for *a true equality* based upon duality of nature and function.

So long as we remain true, speaking broadly, to the fundamental idea of the bi-polarity of society as given by Nature, our feet are planted upon firm ground. The more closely we keep to this position, the more easily we can avoid unwholesome competition between men and women. But in attempting to establish an unnatural identity of function, we open the door to every sort of rivalry and conflict, where there should be harmony and co-operation.

It is because we have no clear social philosophy giving expression in *theory* to the bi-polarity which is always existent in *reality* that we have gradually drifted into the present muddle. On the one hand, there is the tradition of sex distinction, which is still embodied in our legal system (for example, in the husband's obligation to support his wife); on the other, a complex of vague theories of sex equality, which have just enough influence to break down the tradition (for example, in respect of securing the entry of women into various fields of work), but which stop short of effecting any real reconstruction of society on the basis of equality, because, not being founded in reality, these theories prove impracticable when it is sought to apply them with full consequence. We are torn in two between the idea of an abstract sex equality and the actual tendencies of human life, which resist this equality.

Is there, then, any solution at all to the problem of sex equality? Along the line of doctrinaire equalitarianism—No. The idea of an abstract equality, divorced from the whole question of the respective functions and capacities of men and women, is a will-o'-the-wisp leading us into an endless morass of confusion.

But if we attempt to estimate these capacities and to relate them to the life of the community in such a fashion that each sex contributes to the common good that service which best corresponds to its own inherent nature and function, then we are striking out a line which can lead us to *a true equality*, an equality based upon *the realities of life* and not upon vague theories. It is a question of creating for each sex opportunities of life and development which, although different, will be equal in value (moral and financial), and will in each case be such as to correspond to the inner needs of the human being. This true equality will come from within, and not from without; from the nature of being, and not from the abstractions of the intellect. It will be organic, and not rationalistic.

CHAPTER VII

MAN AND WOMAN

a. INTRODUCTORY

THE foregoing chapter should have made it clear that a large part of all our modern discussion of questions concerning men and women is a mere beating of the wind, since the disputants do not trouble to define their terms. The controversy proceeds for the most part through an interchange of empty catchwords. It is therefore of central importance that we should clarify our ideas as to the nature of sex distinction, and decide what we really mean by man and woman, before attempting to deal with Woman and Society.

If we were to accept the view that sex distinction has no importance, and that we may safely, in education and occupation, regard girls precisely as if they were boys, it would be a waste of time to write a book about Woman and Society. For woman, in any significant sense of the term, would then have ceased to exist. The victory of masculinism would be absolute. It could not, for example, matter in the least whether women were or were not represented on public bodies or in political life. If women do not differ from men in psychology as well as in physique, what possible purpose can there be in having women representatives? Men representatives will clearly do just as well!

If feminists were logical, they would at once perceive that their sexless philosophy entirely cuts away the ground from under their own feet when they claim, for example, that women will improve morality, work for peace, or better social conditions, when they have more power. This claim must rest upon the belief that women are, in some very important way, mentally different from men, since it is urged that they will do all sorts of things that men have not done! And yet it is precisely these same feminists who are concerned, on every occasion, to deny that there is any vital difference at all, mentally or morally, between women and men, and resent very attempt, such as is made in this chapter, to elucidate the nature of sex distinctions, as if there were something insulting in the mere idea that women differ at all from men!

In *Woman and Labour*, for example, we find that in one section it is argued that there is really no definable mental difference between men and women; but in another chapter it is urged that if women had power they would abolish war, and in general introduce a new spirit into human affairs![1]

Regarding the matter thus, it is clear that a grave disservice has been done to the woman's cause by those who refuse to face the question of sex psychology. In this way, not only is the position and weight of women representatives undermined, but the Movement deliberately places itself across the path of science. For modern biology and psychology have shown, in illuminating fashion, the depth and significance of sex distinction throughout the whole of life. It is quite impossible that the true interests of women can ever be promoted by those who persist in regarding them as if they were not vitally different from men. The more we explore the rich field of comparative psychology the more we see how characteristic and how deeply significant is the rôle which Nature has assigned to woman, and the more important it must appear that women should neither be suppressed in their development nor side-tracked along masculine lines.

.   .   .   .   .

It is an astonishing fact that so many present-day writers

[1] In *The Cause*, by Mrs. Strachey, the most recent contribution of importance to the literature of our subject, the problem of sex distinction is again passed over.

are able to admit the physical and nervous differences between men and women without apparently realising that these *must* have their corollaries in the mental and emotional sphere. Their desire to believe that, although the sexes differ physically, they are otherwise identical, is so strong that they have allowed themselves to be led into a position that is intrinsically untenable. For the whole teaching of physiology in its connection with psychology demonstrates convincingly that there is (at any rate in *this* life) an indissoluble relationship between mind and body. It is virtually impossible to say where the one begins and the other ends. Human mentality is not an isolated entity disconnected from its physical habitat. It is bound up with the frame in which it dwells.

The basic error of the doctrinaire equalitarians lies in their assumption (implicit, if not always explicit) that mental and emotional characteristics and attributes exist, as it were, *in vacuo*, that they have no organic connection with the person exhibiting them. Their entire ideology is in truth a denial, by implication, of the parallelism which exists between the physical and the psychical. Thus they have no difficulty in believing that a woman may possess a mentality exactly the same as that of a man, although her physical structure is dissimilar. Such doctrine flies in the face of science. Consider, for example, the astonishing influence exerted upon the mind by the secretions of the ductless glands, which are, of course, not the same in the two sexes. The study of these glands is one of the most fascinating chapters in psychology, and it shows us how intimate and delicate is the interaction between our mental life and our bodily functions. How profound, then, must be the reactions in the mental and emotional sphere of the deep organic dissimilarities between men and women!

Is this a confession of materialism? Certainly not. The

K

mutual relationship of mind and body can be explained just as well by assuming that mind is the central reality and that the body is the instrument of the spirit, as by the materialistic view that mind is wholly dependent upon matter. In neither case can we overlook the part played by organic differences in the manifestation of reality.

It is the prevalence of an utterly unpsychological rationalism, a survival from the early days of feminism, that enables us to understand the otherwise almost unaccountable obliviousness of so many writers on women's questions to the above view-point, convincing as it must be to those whose approach is from the side of natural science. It may be some years before we can emancipate ourselves from these Victorian influences. In the meantime progress will be held up for lack of a view-point doing justice to the actual facts of life as regards these questions.

It has always been characteristic of ages of swiftly changing values that the most obvious truths, the most everyday truisms, cease to convince, and have to be re-demonstrated. Nay, more: this denial of the validity of hitherto generally accepted truths is often held to be a mark of progress, when in reality it is only evidence of confusion of thought.

As A. M. Ludovici remarks, in *Man : An Indictment* (p. 41), it is only the popular denial of the fact that men and women must differ mentally as they do physically which makes it necessary to devote time and trouble to demonstrating the obvious. He states the position in the following terms: "Specialised functions, associated with structural differences between organisms, are, and always must be, accompanied by special instincts, emotions, and mental powers."

It is the aim of this chapter to elucidate, at any rate roughly, the problem of woman's special instincts, emotions, and powers.

By way of caution, it must be emphasised that there is not, and cannot be, such a thing as a clear-cut scheme. It is impossible to put all men or all women into any one category. Just as the colour yellow in the solar spectrum merges imperceptibly into red, so the qualities of the one sex merge into those of the other. Nevertheless, just as there *is* a colour yellow and a colour red, even when they cannot easily be separated, there is a normal masculine psychology and there is a normal feminine psychology, in spite of a large army of exceptions and of individuals whose characteristics are vague. The point is that we must take a sufficiently large number of cases in order to establish the rule.

Let us consider a very simple example : speaking generally, it may be said truly that men are taller than women; but this does not mean that every individual man is taller than every individual woman. It might be possible to collect a thousand women, all of whom were taller than the usual man; but this would not prove anything, because we all know that given a large enough field of experiment it can always be shown that men are taller than women. If we were to measure all the men in any given city and compare them with all the women in the same city, it would be found invariably that the men were taller than the women; or, if we were to take at random a hundred women and compare them with a hundred men taken at random, it would always be found that the men were taller.

The same methods must be employed in estimating mental and emotional differences. It might be easy to find a relatively small number of women who were less intuitive than most men, but such a result could only occur through taking too few examples or taking selected examples. If we were to test the intuitive capacities of all the women in a city, it would be found invariably that the women as a body were more highly intuitive than the men. (For evidence see later.)

It is one of the evils of the present-day lack of exact thinking on all such questions that we find ourselves, in consequence, without any established principles. It is, for example, often stated in feminist literature that no definite sex characteristics other than the physical can be established, because men and women are so highly individualised; also that so-called masculine qualities are often found in women, and *vice versa*. All such statements are utterly misleading because they leave us without any norms or criterions which could serve as guides for the educator or sociologist.[1] They merely amount to an avoidance and obscuring of the real problem of sex psychology and its relation to life and education. One might just as well say that because some women are taller than some men it is impossible to arrive at any clear knowledge with regard to the heights of the sexes!

To take an example: feminists will often point to the success of some girl student in philosophy or logic and triumphantly exclaim: "Now what about the old-fashioned idea that men are the logical sex?" Argument of this sort

[1] A great deal of mystification and confusion has been brought into the question of sex distinction by those who say: "There is a feminine element in every man and a masculine element in every woman; these are so blended that there can be no such thing as a definite psychology of sex." But normally the male in the female is recessive, and *vice versa*. If it ceases to be recessive, abnormal and dangerous psychological conditions may result. For this very reason it is specially important to keep a clear grip of sex distinction, although in many individual cases there may be a background of elements more proper to the other sex. As Dr. C. J. Jung says: "A man can live the feminine in himself, and a woman the masculine in herself. None the less, in man the feminine is in the background, as is the masculine in woman. If one lives out the opposite sex in oneself, one is living in one's own background, and that restricts too much the essential individuality. A man should live as a man, and a woman as a woman." (*The New Adelphi*, September 1928.)

is based upon an insufficient survey of the field of study. It is quite possible that one girl, or twenty girls, may be conspicuously above the male average in logical capacity, just as a number of women may be taller than the average man; but, if a large enough area of observation be taken, it will invariably be found that boys and men are superior to girls and women in tests based upon pure logic—in about the same proportion as the female sex is superior in intuition. It will be seen later in this chapter that this is more than a random statement. It has been shown repeatedly that if a large number of unselected women be compared with unselected men of the same class and education, the women are very distinctly behind the men in such tests.

There exists a large body of evidence, accumulated by strictly objective methods and by investigators of a dozen nationalities working independently of one another, all tending to show that certain definite mental and emotional characteristics, and groups of characteristics, are associated with sex. The last ten years or so has seen a great increase in the amount and weight of this evidence, and we could make no greater mistake than to seek to solve the questions pivoting about woman and her place in society without giving the most careful consideration to recent developments in sex psychology.

b. PHYSICAL SEX DISTINCTIONS

This is not a treatise on physiology, and it is not proposed to take up in any detail the physical differences between the sexes; but by way of approach to the psychological differences it will be useful to mention, in passing, a few points of special significance.

The normal woman of Western civilisation is smaller and lighter (by some 15 to 20 lb.) than the normal man; the muscles are not only absolutely less in weight than those of the man, but also relatively (i.e. the percentage of the total weight taken up by the muscles is smaller in the woman than in the man). There are, too, important differences in the constitution and circulation of the blood, and in the nature and functioning of the ductless glands; and both of these factors are necessarily of great significance with respect both to physique and mentality.

The average height of the North European man is about 5 feet 7 inches; of the woman 5 feet 3 inches. Recent experiments show that the physical strength of young men is related to that of young women in the ratio of 100 to between 70 and 80 (it is of some importance to note that this ratio holds good amongst savage tribes as well as in civilised communities, so that it cannot be maintained that women have lost strength as a result of living unnatural lives).[1]

Amongst Northern races the brain volume of the man is represented by 1,500 to 1,550 c.c., and of the woman by 1,300 to 1,350 c.c. (In the Stone Age the ratio was about 1,600 to 1,400.) One c.c. of male blood contains about half a million more red blood corpuscles than the same volume of female blood.[2]

---

[1] The Olympic Games of August 1928 provided an excellent means of checking the accuracy or otherwise of these estimates, for here the performances of the women athletes of the world were comparable with those of men.

The 800 metres race was won by a man in 111 seconds, and by a woman in 136 seconds.

The 200 metres swimming was covered by men in about 168 seconds, and by women in 191 seconds.

These and other records correspond to a ratio of about 100 to 80 in the physical strength of men and women (it must be remembered that the effort required to reduce a record increases enormously with the shortness of the time).

[2] It is a generally admitted fact that the physical type of the woman resembles that of the child more than that of the man. One may hold

In the past, considerable play was made with the smallness of the female brain as an argument against sex equality, but as Havelock Ellis justly observes, a small brain which functions well may be more efficient than a larger one functioning less well. At the same time, it is probable that the greater brain capacity (in a spatial sense) of the man is responsible, at any rate to some extent, for the immense preponderance of the male sex amongst thinkers and philosophers in all ages and in all races. This seems all the more probable when we examine the difference in form between the male and female brain, a difference often very marked at birth. There is good reason to believe, even in our present stage of incomplete knowledge of the psychology of the brain, that in women those sections of the brain are best developed which are associated more directly with the instinctive and emotional side of personality. That the difference in appearance between the male and female brain at birth (as revealed in photos of dissections) can be very striking indeed would seem to indicate that sex difference is accompanied by differences in brain structure (see, for example, the illustrations in *The Opposite Sexes*, by Dr. Heilbronn).

There is no doubt that these and other differences all have their part to play in Nature's purpose of the continuation of the race. It is probable that if the average female muscular system were developed to the same extent and in the same way as the male, it would absorb too much of the

with Havelock Ellis that this is an arrangement of Nature to fit woman for maternity; or with A. M. Ludovici that it is a form of arrested development; or one may take the view that woman is the racial type, and that man has diverged from type in order to take on a more highly specialised form (the greater variability of the male is a notorious fact). Havelock Ellis and, amongst others, Dr. Oskar Schultze have dealt in detail with the above problem of woman's physical type. To their works the reader is referred for details.

energy which Nature requires for racial purposes. (The muscles of the average man weigh about 45 to 50 lb. as compared with about 25 to 30 lb. for the average woman—a very striking difference indeed, and much greater than the relative difference in weight.)

It is important to distinguish between essential, organic differences and those differences (such as weight and size) which represent merely an average, and to which there are innumerable exceptions. There may be thousands of women whose muscles weigh 50 lb., and there may be thousands of men whose muscles weigh under 30 lb. In all such matters we are dealing merely with a norm which holds more or less good for the vast majority, but which is not absolutely essential to the concept man or woman.

Of much greater significance for our study are the *essential* differences; in the first place, of course, the actual organic differences. It is well known that these deeply influence the mental and emotional life of the individual. The reader is referred to medical literature for particulars of the striking effects upon the mental life of abnormalities in this sphere. The remarkable results of castration (affecting, as it does, the whole life and outlook of the subject) are so notorious as to need no special emphasis. In view of such facts, it becomes very difficult to believe that radical organic distinctions like those between man and woman could exist without producing corresponding deep alterations in the mental and emotional life. It is only by a studied avoidance of this aspect of the sex problem that it is possible to maintain the view that the distinction of sex can exist without any parallel mental distinctions.

Recent years have seen a most remarkable development in our knowledge of the complicated system of the ductless glands and their secretions (endocrinology); and there can be no doubt that this system plays a much larger part than had hitherto been known in determining the growth and also the mental and emotional characteristics of the organism. The study of these secretions forms one of the most important chapters in modern physiological-psychology, and it is clear that they have much to do with the determination of physical and mental sex differences. It is not possible within the limits of this book to give even an outline of this difficult subject, but it is perhaps in respect of the ductless glands, more than in any other field, that we see how inextricably the psychic and the physical are interrelated—the slightest defect in the functioning of these glands may produce mental and emotional changes that are quite startling.

. . . . .

To Professor Wieth-Knudsen (*Feminism*) I am indebted for the following quotation from the Norwegian medical authority, Dr. Winge: "The difference of sex is absolutely fundamental, not only in a physical sense, but also mentally; the difference between the typical man and the typical woman is basic. It is not only the sex organs that are different." And again: "The physiological processes in the man are not identical with those in the woman." And Dr. Wieth-Knudsen himself remarks: " . . . man and woman are not equal; they never have been, and they never will be. On the contrary, the difference of sex is so deepgoing, that two men of different civilised races are much more nearly similar in their nature than are a man and woman belonging to the same race."

In *Woman and Labour* we find Olive Schreiner making the rather dangerous admission (from her point of view!) that, "with sexes as with races, it may be that the subtlest physical differences between them may have their fine mental correlatives". Commenting upon this passage, Dr. Arabella

Kenealy writes (in *Feminism and Sex Extinction*, p. 220):
"Men and women are unlike not only in the 'subtlest
physical differences' which 'may have their fine mental
correlatives'. They are unlike in the most obvious and
basic facts of physical constitution and of biological function.
And these must inevitably entail mental and temperamental
correlatives more intrinsic and farther reaching even than
the subtler physical differences she recognises as being
possibly modifying factors in psychical aptitude."

An up-to-date and impartial summing-up of the main
sex differences is to be found in Dr. Heilbronn's little book,
The Opposite Sexes (published by Methuen). In chapter ii he
exposes the absurdity of the view (of which Mme de Staël
was one of the earliest known exponents) that sex distinctions
can be regarded as purely physical and without decisive
mental influence, and points out that there is an inevitable
connection between the physical and psychic lives of individuals, and that the specific mentality of woman is of
necessity correlated with her distinctive structure of body,
brain, and nerve.

The above quotations are given as typical examples of
scientific opinion. They could be multiplied by hundreds.[1]

[1] A popular, and yet thoroughly scientific, brief account of sex
differences is *Sex*, by Professors Patrick Geddes and J. A. Thomson, from
which I take the following extracts:
"While there are undoubtedly differences between man and woman
which are modificational or nurtural—the individual results of dis-
parities or peculiarities in their education, training, and occupations—
many of the differences are constitutional; inborn, not made. They
are intrinsic, not tacked on; of ancient origin, and therefore not liable
to change quickly. They have a deep naturalness, and attempts to
minimise them are not likely to spell progress. . . . As Havelock
Ellis says: 'A man is a man to his very thumbs, and a woman is a woman
down to her little toes.' . . . The differences are correlated, they hang
together, they are outcrops of the deep fundamental distinction. We
may say that the tenacity of life, the longer life, the characteristic
endurance, the greater resistance to disease, the smaller percentage of

For a detailed account of this aspect of the problem the reader is referred to the writings of Havelock Ellis.

The differences in the structure of the nervous system, as between men and women, are of particular importance in their connection with education and occupation. This complicated subject cannot be taken up here; but it may be remarked, in passing, that in the normal woman the sympathetic nervous system (which in the female is connected with important internal organs non-existent in the male) plays a larger part than with the man—an observation which fits in with the general conception of woman's psychology unfolded in this chapter.

c. PSYCHOLOGICAL SEX DISTINCTIONS

If we continually bear in mind the different rôles which the sexes have played down the great perspective of human history, we shall not fail to secure the proper point of view for our purpose. Each sex has its own biological history, and this is stamped in the present make-up of each. It would be as impossible to alter, at this time of day, the qualities which man and woman have acquired, as the result of millions of years of development, as it would be to alter any other product of evolution, such as the habit of going on two

genius, insanity, idiocy, suicide, and crime, and so on, are all correlated with the distinctively female constitution, which may be theoretically regarded as relatively more constructive in its protoplasmic metabolism." Paraphrasing this statement, one may say that the female organism has been admirably adapted by Nature for her racial task of maternity, which demands an immense metabolic effort; while man, with his tendency to externalise his energy, has been fitted for the work of the world. "Man is more given to experiment both with his body and his mind and with other people; man uses more oxygen and combustible material, and has more waste in consequence; man's blood has a higher specific gravity, more red blood corpuscles, more hæmoglobin; man is the relatively more active type."

legs. As Huxley said: "What has been decided amongst pre-historic protozoa cannot be cancelled by Parliament."

In the course of evolution the male of the species has had occasion to develop his cerebro-spinal nervous system more than the female has developed hers, since her functions have been such as to develop the sympathetic nervous system more especially.[1] In accordance with this biological history, the female is normally swifter and more sensitive in her reactions to emotions (such as joy, fear, grief, or hope). Her greater sensibility, while a valuable quality, tends to make her unstable and subjective. It is a truism to say that women are more influenced by their feelings (say, in their judgment of individuals) than are men. All these

---

[1] It is sometimes sought to weaken the force of this line of argument by raising the question of inheritance through the father. It is said: "Do not girls inherit from their fathers as much as from their mothers; and accordingly is it not a fact that so-called male characteristics will tend to be passed on to daughters? How, then, can it be said that a certain type of nervous system or of mentality can be passed down by women through the ages?" These points have a certain air of plausibility. But it must be remembered that there is the closest connection between physical structure and psychic characteristics. It will be admitted that the male physique, as such, is not inherited by daughters from their fathers, otherwise they would not be daughters at all. The male type of nervous system could not exist in the female body. Similarly, the system of the ductless glands is, in the father, definitely male. The composition of the blood is also male. The same with a dozen other physical characteristics. And all these peculiarities of structure have their mental correlations; so that a given girl cannot inherit from her father any part of his mental make-up that is definitely male, i.e. organically linked up with his physical structure. And what she can inherit will be remodelled in accordance with the demands and limitations of the organism in which this inherited element now finds itself at home. The specifically masculine element in the inheritance of a daughter comes into a dwelling highly uncongenial to its nature, one in which, in fact, it cannot possibly expand to full development because the necessary organic basis is lacking. It thus remains recessive, or develops within such narrow limits as to lose its character and become feminised.

qualities follow from the general structure of the female organism. If women possessed a nervous system identical with that of the male, they would be totally unfitted for their maternal functions. Paradoxically, women, although more emotional[1] than men, are able, as is well known, to bear pain much better, and possess in general a superior capacity of resisting suffering and illness (hence the notorious higher mortality of boy babies). This, again, is part of Nature's scheme. It has often been truly said that if men had to bear the children of the race, we should soon be hastening towards extinction. The remarkable vitality and passive endurance of women is needful for the survival of the race. The paradox by which women are outwardly more sensitive than men, while really possessing more endurance, is explained by the greater elasticity and adaptability of the female nervous system.[2] When confronted with some danger, such as a fire or a violent storm, women as a rule show the outward signs of fear or disturbance much sooner than men—in a street panic women nearly always faint in greater numbers than men. All this is natural when we consider the peculiar structure of the female organism. Yet, when put to the point of enduring any trial of vital force, women will generally come through better than men, which is explained by their inherited capacity for passive endurance.

The above may be placed in another light by saying that, broadly speaking, the subconscious and instinctive aspects of human personality are stronger in women, while the conscious and rational side is much more developed in men. Outwardly, the man, whose reactions are more controlled than the woman's, shows less sign of fear or disturbance;

[1] For a note on the exact meaning of "emotional", see p. 191.
[2] It is an interesting fact that long-distance swimming, which needs endurance rather than strength, is the only athletic exercise in which women can come near the records set up by men.

but owing to his inferior instinctive power he finds it more difficult to survive, for example, an exhausting operation than would a woman. As a doctor has expressed it: the woman faces the operation showing every sign of perturbation and alarm, but survives; the man clenches his teeth, shows no outward signs of fear, and—dies!

It will be shown later how weighty is the evidence in support of the general thesis that women excel in the subjective, instinctive, intuitional, and emotional aspects of human life; while men, on the other hand, are objective, rational, abstract, and analytical. If women have more passive endurance, men have more initiative. The chief strength of the male lies in his superior originality and initiative. And both of these qualities are corollaries of the masculine power of detachment—of man's ability to stand outside and above his work and functions, as well as within them.

It has been well said that man is for the race, but woman *is* the race. The masculine characteristics are those useful for the work of the world—practical energy, reasoning power, scientific sense, initiative, will-power; the feminine characteristics are those necessary for the preservation of the race—maternal instinct, selfless devotion, patience, cheerful endurance, adaptability to circumstances, sympathy, intuition.

"Her whole soul, conscious and unconscious, is best conceived as a magnificent organ of heredity, and to its laws all her psychic activities, if unperverted, are true."—Dr. Stanley Hall, *Adolescence*, chapter xvii.

Mr. A. M. Ludovici hits the nail square on the head when he says (in *Woman: A Vindication*) that woman's chief attributes are those which "make for a continuance of the human species on earth", and as being "of so much moment . . . that they overshadow every catalogue of foibles or vices that has ever been drawn up against her by a Weininger or a Schopenhauer".

From this point of view many seemingly enigmatical things become clear and obvious. The popular idea that women are cowardly and weak as compared with men is at once refuted by the fact that women will show incredible courage on behalf of anyone to whom they are attached. As a matter of fact, there is some truth both in the popular idea and in its refutation. The preservation of the species requires from woman, on the one hand, that she should be cautious and fearful to a degree, in order that she may be constantly on the look out for danger threatening her beloved offspring or mate; and on the other, that she should be as bold as a female tiger in defence of, or devotion to, man or child; and woman, being far nearer to Nature than man, responds with ease to demands apparently so incompatible. The pages of history and the experience of our daily lives abound with examples of women who have displayed, when it was called for, a truly astounding courage and stoicism (such as that exhibited by the heroic women of the Indian Mutiny days), and yet who were, in their daily life, ultra-feminine in the early Victorian sense of the term —that is, nervous, sensitive, emotional, and easily liable to tears. (Cf. also the heroines in Shakespeare's plays.)

It is, in fact, precisely this plasticity of character, this ready transition from one state of mind to another according to the demands of the moment, which is so typical of the normal woman. It is part of the adaptability which Nature has developed in the female for racial purposes. The firm, rational, strong-willed, independent type of woman who is no rarity to-day is, in reality, a departure from the normal feminine. She is the product of a highly artificial system of life and education. She will, in all probability, prove to be an evolutionary reject.

There is nothing more valuable in Mr. Ludovici's striking analysis of the female character than his demonstration that the so-called "weaknesses" of woman, as known to tradition and popular opinion, are in reality only a part of her natural strength, an essential element in her equipment for her racial tasks. Consider, for example, how much selfless adaptation is needed for the care of young children, how much pliability, sympathy, and intuition, and how few men there are (if any) who would be capable of exercising these qualities! But such qualities could scarcely be developed at all save through a type of nervous system and mentality inferior to the masculine in other antithetical qualities, such as independence, will-power, firmness, self-assertion, or a high capacity for abstract thought. The modern idea that women must remain inferior to men, unless they can develop these latter qualities, and others of a similar nature, rests upon an over-valuation of the masculine side of life, which, as I have more than once urged, is one of the evils of the present age of science and machinery. In the Middle Ages, for example, the unique value and significance of the typically feminine qualities was far more widely appreciated than is now the case.[1]

.   .   .   .   .

One of the many evil results of modern equalitarian doctrines is that public opinion is thereby led to value and judge women by the prevailing (i.e. masculine) standards,

[1] It is very significant that Havelock Ellis draws attention to the under-valuation of the specifically feminine qualities which has accompanied the growth of militarism and nationalism in Europe since the close of the Middle Ages. With militant nationalism goes the worship of the typically masculine qualities suited to the soldier, pioneer, or nationalist politician. On the other hand, the moral and religious atmosphere of the earlier period was favourable to a higher valuation of many typically feminine characteristics. When militant nationalism is combined (as in the modern world) with industrialism, we have an atmosphere which might be described as ideally anti-feminine.

with the result that woman's real character is completely misunderstood. Seen in its true light, as racially needful and as essentially complementary (and not similar) to man's character, it acquires at once *a higher position and a truer understanding*. At present woman suffers heavily from the circumstance that she is expected to justify herself according to standards that are not her own.

The charges of hyper-emotionalism and erratic subjectivity which have from time immemorial been brought against woman are traceable to qualities inseparable from her close intimacy with Nature. Man stands, as it were, outside Nature, and can contemplate it with detachment. But woman is so bound up with the heart of Nature—presiding, as she does, at the altars of birth and death—that it is idle to expect from her the philosophical objectivity which comes comparatively easily to a man. Nothing could be more foolish than these charges of fickleness, emotionalism, and general instability which have for so long been brought against woman. They could emanate only from persons too superficial to understand the true function of woman in society and the necessity she is under to obey inner laws unknown to man.

In her essence, woman is the incarnation of "the will-to-live". Primarily concerned with the creation and nurture of life itself in the flesh, it would be strange indeed if she could stop to elaborate the abstract rules and norms which seem to men so important; and for this reason woman often acts in what, to the male, seems a wilful and irresponsible fashion, although perhaps in this very moment she is most of all obeying the will of her mistress, Nature.

> The man's a fool who tries by force or skill
> To stem the current of a woman's will;
> For if she will, she will, you may depend on't,
> And if she won't, she won't, and there's an end on't.

L

A vast amount of friction between the sexes is due to the fact that men rely upon *reason*, while women are actuated by motives drawn from *the subconscious*. It thus appears to the man that the woman is unreasonable, whimsical, and erratic, and he becomes impatient at her imperviousness to his rational arguments. On the other hand, the woman finds male reason pedantic, absurd, and unreal. The remedy for such friction is better understanding between the sexes, but this can be brought about only through true psychological insight, and not through the education of women along masculine lines. With such insight each sex should learn to respect and value the specific attributes of the other. One of the worst results of the current levelling-down of distinctions in this sphere is that this healthy mutual respect is undermined.

In its place we get the cult of an unnatural equality, which so far from bringing the sexes nearer together forces them apart. For the attraction of the sexes for one another is the age-long need of woman by man, and of man by woman, the search for the self-complementary opposite, for the personality who will fulfil the lack in self. Taking up this standpoint, it is easy enough to understand the curious atmosphere of sex antipathy which is so noticeable in the Anglo-Saxon lands.[1] For when the mentality of either man or woman begins to be dominated by a false idea of sex equality, at once trouble creeps in. Every little difference in position or privilege, real or apparent, immediately becomes a ground for envy or resentment, instead of appearing as part of the natural order of things.[2]

   .   .   .   .   .

Nothing could better illustrate the superficiality of the

[1] Cf. H. G. Wells, *The World of William Clissold*, vi, 1 : "I cannot help but recognise the atmosphere of intensifying sex antagonism in which we are living."

[2] In an article in the *Spectator* (March 5, 1927), Miss King-Hall

"levelling", rationalist-utilitarian outlook upon these matters than a comparison between the verdict spoken from this standpoint upon the subject of sex difference and the verdict spoken from the far deeper and more truthful standpoint of *feeling and intuition* as interpreted in great works of art.

However much our doctrinaire equalitarians may advocate the idea of sex equality as a theoretical proposition, not one of them would venture to commit the absurdity of modelling a pair of ideal figures in which the woman was the same height as the man. In art it has always been recognised that, although there are plenty of women who are, in fact, taller than men, this is not the right relationship from an æsthetic standpoint; and in every artistic representation of a human couple, the distinction of sex *must* be shown, not only in the varying forms of the figures, but also in a subordination of the female figure to that of the male—otherwise the effect upon the mind of the spectator (even of a feminist spectator!) would be catastrophic. This would seem to indicate that, however much the idea of sex equality has influenced the intellect of the modern world, it has not penetrated to the deeper subconsciousness which pronounces an instinctive æsthetic judgment. It might be objected to this argument that the mere fact of the female figure being smaller or lighter than the male is nothing against the idea of sex equality. In a purely physical sense this may be so; but the point of my argument

describes very accurately some of the leading characteristics of the present-day English girl, and refers to the curious mixture of *camaraderie* and "latent sex hostility" which marks her attitude towards her young men friends. The lack of any deeper understanding of sex difference in nature and function is probably the main cause both of this hostility and of the general "aggressiveness" of the modern girl. Our schools are seriously to blame for their failure to give the growing girl a correct orientation towards this side of life.

is that a work of art portraying men and women would
entirely fail of its effect if the grouping of the figures did
not convey a certain air of leadership and authority in the
male figures and suggest something of antithetical qualities
in the female figures. A statue of a pair in which the woman
was equal to the man in height, and expressed in her pose
the same mental characteristics as the man, would produce
an effect that would be simply grotesque. It could not be
set up anywhere. Not even in the lobby of a building housing
an organisation of militant feminists! Is it not possible that
the subconscious instinct which would cause this work to be
instantly laughed out of existence is really a far truer guide
than the rationalistic theories which support the idea of sex
equality? Or, in other words, is not the whole idea of
equality (in the cheap, popular sense) simply a product of
the half-baked intellectualism of the age—a thing which is
seen to be an absurdity when looked at from another
angle?

In just the same way we may argue that no literary work
which attempted to carry out the idea of sex equality (in a
psychological sense) in the treatment of the characters
and events would be read by anybody. It would be too
manifestly a manufactured article. Let us take the great
women writers. One and all they show us in their works
women characters who are mentally and spiritually wholly
different from the men. It does not matter whether we
think of George Eliot's pictures of the Victorian world, or
whether we take a quite modern authoress, such as Margaret
Kennedy. Since an author is compelled, if his work is not
to be a fiasco, to take some notice of reality, he must show
people more or less as they actually are, and accordingly
no writer pays the slightest attention to the idea of sex
equality. In one of the cleverest recent novels, *The Constant
Nymph*, we have a study, as true as it is amusing, of a number

of modern girls and men, in which many fundamental feminine characteristics are shown in a somewhat exaggerated form. Another of our greatest women writers, Edith Wharton, has given us portraits of a series of modern girls, not one of whom could by any conceivable chance be a man in respect of her mental and moral attributes.

If I were to refer to Jane Austen, I should expose myself to the charge of Victorianism; but I am not afraid to maintain that there is more knowledge of human life in her books than in all the manifestoes of our women's organisations put together. As a matter of fact, it is unimportant where we look. Jane Eyre, with her "Wherever you are, sir, is my home", was not less of an equalitarian than almost any heroine of a modern novel, if we consider the fundamental attributes of the latter, and not her acquired life-outlook. A novelist cannot be a doctrinaire; and the moment we leave the study and step into real life, all the artificial theories of the equalitarians are blown away by the fresh wind of experience and concrete reality.

For this reason a course of novel-reading is a wholesome antidote to the arm-chair theories of our equalitarian fanatics. Thackeray is a better guide than John Stuart Mill, and Edith Wharton knows a great deal more about life than Mrs. C. P. Gilman does. A study of the works of Meredith, Galsworthy, Edith Wharton, and W. B. Maxwell—to take four leading psychological novelists—would be an excellent introduction to sex psychology, and from their female characters the reader might very well deduce practically all the attributes and qualities of womanhood which are expounded in this chapter.

Must we not see that the equalitarianism of to-day is the child of an utterly one-sided rationalism, of a life-outlook which is lacking in depth and instinct, and has no roots in the subconscious life of humanity?

d. Genius and Sex

In *Women and Economics*, Mrs. C. P. Gilman is much concerned to persuade us that if little girls were dressed and educated exactly like little boys, they would lose their sex characteristics and virtually become boys (it is *not*, of course, suggested that, by a reverse process, boys might become girls, since, like nearly all other doctrinaire feminists, Mrs. Gilman does not attach any importance to the feminine side of life!). It is the constant suggestion given to Mary that she must behave like a girl, that it is the proper thing that she should play with a doll, while her little brother draws a locomotive about the floor, that creates the feminine mentality. Such a view entirely overlooks the whole question of mentality in its relation to structure, and flies in the face of obvious biological truths in the field of heredity and instinct.

By way of corollary to this theory it is maintained that if women in the past have played a part inferior to that of men in art, literature, politics, science, or philosophy, it is simply and solely because they have been deprived of opportunity, because of *the condition of subjection* in which they have been held.

It is rather difficult to believe that this argument is taken altogether seriously even by those who advance it.

It is, of course, quite untrue that men have invariably throughout history enjoyed better opportunities for mental and cultural development. For a very lengthy period during the Middle Ages women had opportunities of study and of mental betterment in general which were superior to those enjoyed by the men of the period. Ellen Key, the well-known Swedish feminist, admitted freely that for at least a thousand years large numbers of women throughout Europe enjoyed opportunities for culture in art, literature, and music far more favourable than those of their menfolk, who were almost wholly absorbed in war, politics, commerce, and agriculture. Nevertheless, nearly all the leading artists, writers, poets, and musicians of this period were of the male sex. If it were really true that sex has nothing to do with genius or talent, we should have expected in this period to see women taking the first place in the arts and studies which they more especially cultivated, while men led in war, politics, commerce, and agriculture.

Or to come to more modern times: during the last hundred years or so, in England or in many other Western lands, there has been an abundance of opportunity for women to produce noteworthy achievements in art, literature, or music. In Victorian England there were thousands upon thousands of leisured women, possessed of ample means, with nothing in the world to hinder their success in any branch of creative work they chose to pursue. In what way were these women so handicapped that their potentialities could not come to expression? The argument that their education was insufficient is invalid for two reasons: in the first place, genuine original work in the arts and in literature does not depend upon education—many of the foremost men geniuses never had any educational advantages; in the second place, the educational drawbacks of the Victorian woman have been grossly exaggerated for propaganda purposes. Many women of the upper classes had an excellent education. It would be easy to gather the names of numerous women of this period who were as well grounded in the classics, in modern languages, and in the arts, as any of their men relations.

Again, in eighteenth-century France, it is well known that women played a prominent part in cultural life, and frequently received the very best educational advantages obtainable. Many of these women were world-famous for their wit and intellect. But the really outstanding literary and artistic achievements of the period must nevertheless be placed to the credit of the male sex.

Further, supposing we were to grant, for the sake of argument, that women have been suppressed and thwarted, this could scarcely be taken as an explanation of their failure to equal men in the production of great works of the mind. For is it not a notorious fact that a very large proportion of the most eminent men were themselves born and reared in the most disadvantageous environment? It was the mark of their supreme genius that it triumphed over every hindrance offered by a hostile world. Socrates, St. Paul, Leonardo da Vinci, Dickens, Burns, Dostoievsky, and a host of others, rose victorious over the most adverse circumstances. What valid reason is there why women in past ages, even in those ages in which women really were held in subjection, should not, like these great men, have risen superior to all difficulties, supposing that the genuine stuff of genius had been in them? If a Socrates can secure immortal fame as a philosopher while living as an obscure handworker, there does not appear to be any reason why a housewife, in the midst of her pots and pans, should not also revolutionise philosophy, granted an equal measure of original genius.

It is sufficient to review a few of the names that have made history to perceive how overwhelmingly predominant the masculine mind has been in all the main fields of human development.

In philosophy we may recall Socrates, Plato, Thomas Aquinas, Descartes, Kant, Hegel, Schopenhauer, Darwin, Nietzsche, and Bergson. In art: Phidias, Michel Angelo, Leonardo da Vinci, Titian, Velasquez, and Rembrandt. In music: Bach, Mozart, Beethoven, and Wagner. In literature: Homer, Virgil, Dante, Chaucer, Shakespeare, Bacon,

Milton, Molière, Balzac, Goethe, Dickens, Dostoievsky, and Ibsen. In the religious development of the race: Confucius, Buddha, Paul, Mohammed, Augustine, Luther, Calvin, and Fox.

I refrain from mentioning science or war, since in these fields it is true that there has been little opportunity for women. It is quite natural that almost the only women whose names really stand out in history are those of great queens (such as Cleopatra and Elizabeth), or of great religious personalities (such as Joan of Arc, St. Catherine of Genoa, or St. Elizabeth of Thuringia), since in the field of politics, where a knowledge of human nature plays a great part, or in the sphere of religion, where women have special gifts, we should expect to find that women would make a good showing. It is in fact surprising that women, with their innate faculty for dealing with people and situations, should not have played an even more conspicuous part in politics. But in order to estimate the real influence of women in politics it would be needful to peruse the most secret pages of history.

The reader may put forward such names as Jane Austen, Charlotte Brontë, or George Eliot, in literature. But to place these side by side with Dante, Shakespeare, or Goethe is to reveal only too clearly that even the foremost representatives of feminine genius cannot claim equal rank with the epoch-making minds of history. They come high in the second class, but they cannot fairly be given a place in the first class. In the long run the plain truth will serve us all much better than tendencious efforts to assign to women writers or artists a place above their real merit.

It is at first sight surprising that women should not take a much higher place than they do in music, seeing that for so long music has played a special part in the education of girls. In this sphere, at any rate, no one could by any chance contend that women have not had an equal chance. Yet in spite of the great skill of many women as performers, the sex as a whole would seem to be remarkably deficient in the capacity to originate great music. Rubinstein once commented on the fact that no woman had ever written even one of the classical cradle songs or love duets. In the musical world we see in fact with peculiar clearness that there must be some real defect of creative power in the feminine psychology. Otherwise it is hard indeed to account for the fact that in a field where for centuries they have had every possible chance, and in which it is admitted that as executants they reach the highest level, they have nevertheless not contributed any names to the list of really great composers of music.

With regard to pictorial art, too, it would be difficult to maintain the thesis that women have been fatally hampered by their sex. During the Middle Ages, for example, there were countless nunneries in which illuminating and painting were highly developed, and yet it must be admitted that all the outstanding names in the history of art are those of men. Although able to reach a high level of technical merit, it would seem, here too, as if women were deficient in the quality of originality needed to produce works of the highest artistic genius. If anyone at all (even the most convinced feminist!) were to make a list of the hundred greatest paintings or statues of history, it is scarcely possible that even one would be the work of a woman artist.

In accordance with the foregoing analysis of male and female characteristics it would be expected that women would sink very much into the background in philosophy. And such is indeed the case. The power of abstract thought required in the philosophical world is in a very special degree a masculine quality. No woman has ever attained even to second-class eminence in this field of work. It is a

comparatively rare thing for a girl student to do even
moderately well in any philosophical subject. The capacity
for impersonal, objective thought runs wholly contrary to
the bias of the typical feminine mentality, which is overwhelmingly personal and subjective, so that in the masculine
monopoly of the field of philosophy we find a fresh corroboration of the general accuracy of the position outlined above
with regard to sex qualities.

On the other hand, the stage offers an opportunity for the
display of some of the most characteristic feminine qualities,
such as intuition, quickness of apprehension, control of
voice and gesture, emotional intensity, sense of rhythm,
interest in human phenomena, penetration into character,
swift adaptability to changing situations, endurance and
patience; and nothing would seem more probable than that
women should achieve their greatest successes in the theatre.
In every age since women have appeared upon the stage
they have scored amazing triumphs. It is, indeed, doubtful
whether any man has ever reached quite the level of the
greatest actresses.

Taking their stand upon the foregoing facts, certain
unintelligent champions of male superiority have asserted,
in their shortsightedness, that practically the whole of
human culture is the work of men. Stupid and narrow-
minded as this assertion is, it has done much to obscure the
real facts of the case. Justly enraged women have retorted
by setting up their impossible equalitarian theories. In this
controversy neither side shows any capacity to perceive the
true relationships which lie behind the phenomena.

It is unquestionably true that practically all the epoch-
making personalities in art, music, literature, philosophy,
and science have been men. It has even been maintained

that if all that women have contributed *directly* to the edifice of our mental culture and civilisation were removed, the building would remain almost intact; whereas we have only to consider the contributions of such men as Plato, Shakespeare, Kant, Goethe, or Darwin to perceive that their removal would leave the whole fabric of culture in ruins.

But even if, for the sake of argument, we were to accept the latter statement, which puts the matter in its most extreme form, this would afford no justification whatever for the stupid and narrow-minded view we have mentioned.

We have only to ask the one question, What would these men have achieved *alone*, without the co-operation and assistance of women? to reveal the utter lack of intelligent insight in this view. In the first place it will, I presume, be admitted that all these men had mothers. The commanding part that has been played in the lives of a very large proportion of great men by their mothers is so well known that it is superfluous to mention it.[1] It is often impossible to draw a line between what a man owes to himself and what he owes to the influence of his mother. If we take a broader view of life than that of the nineteenth-century individualists (whose erroneous philosophy has done so much to cloud all the issues discussed in this book), it is easy to see that it is, in reality, utterly impossible to draw any boundary between feminine and masculine influence in the development of civilisation. Not only have all these great men had mothers, but the vast majority of them have had wives, mistresses, sisters, or women friends, whose personalities and influence were so inextricably intertwined with their lives and work that to attribute all that they achieved to male genius shows a complete failure to grasp the complexity and organic

---

[1] Even such ultra-masculine personalities as Napoleon and Mussolini have acknowledged that the influence of their mothers was of fundamental significance.

nature of human relationships. If we were to subtract from the work of (say) Dante, Balzac, or Goethe all that they owed, directly and indirectly, to women relations, friends, or lovers, what remained would be at best an empty framework.

It might be argued further, that even if we were to overlook the immense part played by women in the lives of men of genius, the fact would still remain that women were co-partners in all the achievements of human mentality, if only for the reason that it is impossible to conceive of works of art, music, or literature at all, in the absence of women from human society, since they play an absolutely indispensable rôle as subject-matter and as the objects of inspiration! What would be left of poetry if all the poems written about and around women and love were removed? What would remain of art without its principal objects of representation?

This line of thought could obviously be developed at length, but it is enough to make it clear that the edifice of human culture has been erected through a fruitful co-operation between the sexes, in which it is stupid to ask the question, Who has played the greater part? Human life is a vast network of relationships in which the apparent independence of individuals is an illusion. Just as it is an illusion on the part of feminists to aim at independence as a life-ideal, so it is an illusion on the part of our shortsighted and arrogant masculinists to imagine that the great men of history made their epoch-making contributions to human development as isolated individuals and independent of feminine co-operation.

That noble-minded man and distinguished thinker, the late Professor Friedrich Paulsen, often impressed upon his fellow-countrymen the immense, but far too little recognised, debt that they owed to the unobtrusive and loyal work of the German women of the last century, without whose co-operation the great achievements of scholarship, science, and industry which raised Germany so rapidly to a foremost place amongst the nations would have been impossible. Many a work, he contended, which is attributed to a man should more justly be regarded as a joint effort; for even if his wife, mother, or sister, as the case might be, took no active part in its production, it would be found that she had created, through her devotion and effort, the conditions of life under which alone such work could be done. For, strictly regarded, every work of genius or scholarship is the upshot, not simply of processes going on in the brain of a single individual, but of a certain set of circumstances and a certain constellation of factors; and in the creation of these conditions, if not in the actual intellectual task itself, it will usually be found that some woman has played a commanding rôle. The injustice of which women often very rightly complain lies not so much in the fact that they have been debarred by male tyranny from enjoying equal opportunities (for it was not *opportunity* that enabled Beethoven to create his music, or Kant to write his philosophy!), but that their work of co-partnership in all the great achievements of the race has been so poorly *valued*.

Such a point of view as this will, of course, be met with howls of derision in the feminist camp. Not for a moment do I suggest that any woman who does possess distinguished powers should be prevented from developing them (indeed, as will be seen in the following chapter, a reorganisation of society along organic and functional lines would increase the opportunities of able women); but the fact remains that the number of women who do possess highly original mental ability, as compared with those who are endowed with the traditional feminine qualities, is very small indeed. It is therefore a catastrophic error to aim at fitting girls for exceptional tasks rather than at fitting them for those tasks for which they are naturally gifted. Not one girl in a hundred thousand will ever produce a work of creative intellect which could not have been produced by a man just as well, but more than half the girls in every ordinary school will be capable, if rightly educated, of taking part, indirectly, as wives or mothers (or both), in the general development of the intellectual and spiritual life of the race *in their own specific and indispensable way*—a way which could not be rivalled or substituted by any man, however gifted.

.　　.　　.　　.　　.

We have already touched upon the theory that women have been prevented by masculine oppression from fulfilling their highest mental possibilities, and found it untenable. The true explanation of the overwhelming preponderance of men amongst the great personalities of history is much more simple. A division of labour as between man and woman is obviously part of the scheme of Nature—otherwise we should have had one sex and not two (bi-sexuality is not, of course, essential to propagation).

If women really were possessed of the same mental powers as men in every respect, if man had *nothing* to call his own (which is the view apparently held by feminists of the orthodox persuasion), and if, in addition (as *must* be the case), they were the mothers of the race, women would rule the world. They would be supreme. They would be man's equals in the mental world and his superiors in the physical world (where man is not creative). They would be absolutely unique beings, bi-sexual, while man was uni-sexual. They would possess all man's powers and all woman's powers as well.

It is very interesting to note, in passing, that Mr. Langdon Davies in his *Short History of Women* actually goes so far as to say that, were the intellectual equality of men and women

established, and were women freed from restrictions of every
kind, "women cannot fail to dominate". (To this statement
we shall return shortly.)

But Nature has decreed otherwise. Having bestowed upon
woman the all-important function of motherhood, the
power of creation in the physical plane, she has granted to
man, by way of compensation, a superior power of creation
on the mental plane.

There is nothing artificial about this compensation. It
follows naturally from the evolution of the sexes. Woman has
throughout the generations been heavily handicapped by
her functions of menstruation, parturition, and lactation—
these have hindered her mobility of body and taken up much
of the time during which she might have developed a more
abstract mentality. For thousands of years the average woman
has reared a family of some four or more children. The
childless women, whose opportunities in a purely intellectual
sense have been better, have not passed their qualities on to
future generations, the mentality of the normal child-bearing woman thus being determinative in a hereditary sense.
When we consider how much time and trouble goes to the
upbringing of a family of four children (and in most of the
civilisations of the past the average has been well above
four), we begin to realise the actual severity of the handicap
from which women have suffered. Reckoning roughly, some
ten years, at the very least, has been taken out of the life of
the typical woman—years during which, save in rare cases,
she could not devote herself, with masculine single-mindedness, to things of the mind. Moreover, the loss of time is the
smallest part of the matter. In order to secure the vital force
needful for the children, Nature has drawn upon the physical
resources of each generation of mothers to deflect to racial
purposes power which otherwise might have gone into higher
nerve centres. (This argument is worked out very lucidly

by Mr. Ludovici in *Man : an Indictment*, chapter ii.) The whole matter may be summed up under the head of *the unequal cost of reproduction*. Man's share of the reproductive process costs him little of direct loss of energy (the work which he does to support the family not being reckoned); while woman's share costs her the best years of her life.

In view of the foregoing, how short-sighted is the view which attributes all woman's shortcomings (as judged from the standpoint of masculine values) to male tyranny and oppression! It must be as plain as plain can be that even if women had never at any time suffered from man-made restrictions, they could never (as a body) have developed so precisely along male lines as to have attained the male level of achievement in mental culture. It is superfluous to point out that this achievement is the product of a concentration and detachment, of a specialisation in this department of life, which the female has never enjoyed, for the extremely simple reason that her time and energy have been too much occupied in other directions. It was not domineering man who decreed that the female should bear and feed the young of the species! We are here face to face with ultimate realities which we are powerless to alter. If man has tended to become a specialist in practical initiative and abstract mentality, woman has tended to become a specialist in all the instinctive and emotional qualities which fit her for her racial tasks. The path of progress does not consist in endeavouring to level down these distinctions, but in accepting them as part of the purpose of human life and developing them in ever more and more harmonious forms.

For a moment let us come back to Mr. Langdon Davies. Let me quote him more fully: "Once both sexes use their reasons equally, and have no unequal penalty awaiting the exercise of their emotions, then women cannot fail to dominate. Theirs is the stronger sex once Nature and Art

M

cease their cruel combination against them." I am reminded of once reading in the margin of a book upon sex psychology —at a point where woman's unequal share in the cost of reproduction was attributed to a law of Nature—the scribbled comment, made no doubt by some feminist reader: "Down with Nature!" Down with Nature by all means— if you know how to do it. It is true that women would dominate, *if* they did use their reason equally, *if* they were not the mothers of the race, and *if* Nature, in accordance with her principle of bi-polarity and duality of function, had not weighted the scales against women in the mental field. But what is the good of discussing what women *might* do, *if* the whole structure of human life were quite different from what it is? We have no means of propagating the race, save by the act of maternity, and hence (in the case of any civilisation that is not actually declining) the mass of women *must* be largely taken up with functions from which men are free.

Even John Stuart Mill, who would certainly have written in another sense if it had been possible to do so, admitted that women "have not yet produced any of those great and luminous new ideas which form an era of thought". An objective study of the actual facts must compel to the conclusion that women are, by virtue of their entire racial heredity, less endowed with the special sort of power and originality which renders possible the highest type of intellectual achievement; and this conclusion is strengthened by the observation that, even when all the circumstances are wholly favourable, women do not, as a matter of observed fact, produce original works of genius on a level with those of the other sex.

The impartial reader will find himself brought back to a belief in one of the oldest of truisms—namely, that *a division of labour between the sexes is part of the scheme of evolution.* It is one of the calamities of modern civilisation that this ancient and obvious truth has been placed on the shelf. Many of our greatest difficulties in education and in social life are due to its neglect.

e. The Psychology of Woman

It is hoped that the foregoing sections will serve to clear the ground and give the reader an idea of the general tendencies of psychological sex distinction.

We have no space here for a full account of the psychology of woman. The reader who wishes to pursue this subject more deeply is referred to the invaluable works of Havelock Ellis; *The Nature of Woman*, by Dr. Lionel Tayler; the well-known German works on sex psychology by Tandler and Gross, Bauer, Forel, Hirschfeld, and others; and to A. M. Ludovici's *Woman*. In this chapter it is sought merely to emphasise those attributes of typical womanhood which are significant for our subject—Woman and Society.

The broad lines of sex distinction result inevitably from the specialised functions of the two sexes. Nature has equipped the male to be the father of the race, the female to be the mother of the race. This fact is fixed once and for all in the nature of reality, and it is idle to make a grievance of any limitations which it may entail. The door leading to all the varied and enriching experiences of maternity has been shut for ever to the male sex; and it is not in the least unreasonable if women, too, have to put up with certain limitations imposed upon them by the conditions of human life upon this planet. There is something purely childish in the mentality of those who can write (like a certain feminist of repute) of the sufferings of women in maternity as a "wrong done to woman". A man might just as well say that men have been "wronged" because they cannot enjoy the delights of motherhood (which, according to Olive Schreiner,

are ample compensation for the suffering which often pre-
cedes them!).

The idea, often put forth to-day, that women as a whole,
or certain sections of women, can put the whole tradition
and history of their sex behind them, and by some process of
"emancipation" transcend the order of Nature, becoming
super-beings with no special sex characteristics at all, is
utter nonsense. Apply this idea to the male sex, and its
absurdity is at once revealed. No man, however a-sexual or
feminine in type, could ever transcend his masculinity to
the extent of being able to perform feminine functions. No
man will ever be able to give birth to a child or to suckle
a child. And conversely no woman, however neuter in type,
or however masculinised she may become, will ever be able
to perform paternal functions. But there is an *essential*
connection between the functions themselves and the mental
and emotional characteristics which go along with them.
A man cannot really *equal* a woman in feminine mental
characteristics (however effeminate he may be in his type
as compared with other men) so long as he cannot actually
function along feminine lines. Conversely, a woman cannot
acquire masculine emotional and mental characteristics (in
the fullest sense) because she is debarred from the masculine
functions which are the physiological basis of these mental
qualities. These things are mere truisms. But as I have said
before, so confusing is the sophistry of to-day that they are
truisms needing to be constantly re-emphasised.[1]

· · · · ·

One of the outstanding facts of sex psychology is that *the*

---

[1] Dr. Oskar Schultze, one of the most scientific investigators in this
field, is of the opinion that all students of sex psychology must agree in
attributing to women a superiority over men in the emotional perception of the concrete and individual. He regards these characteristics

centre of gravity of the female mind lies more in the subconscious, that
of the male more in the conscious. It has been observed
from time immemorial that women tend to reach their
conclusions by swift intuitive processes, of the nature of
which they are themselves quite unaware, while men usually
plod along the path of conscious reason. This fact is en-
shrined in one form or another in the phrases and proverbs
of every race under the sun.

Nothing, in fact, is more thoroughly typical of women
than their remarkable sharpness of perception, their rapid
subconscious assimilation of all the facts of a given situation.
They do not stop to think the matter out, but leap at a
bound to the goal. That this is really a native quality of
women is proved especially by the fact that it is quite
independent of education (and often even of other aspects
of intelligence). An ignorant peasant woman will often
astonish us by virtue of the acuteness of her judgment on all
matters connected with personality and character. Indeed,
in this respect the uneducated woman is not infrequently
superior to her cultured sister, whose intellectual development is apt to take place somewhat at the expense of her
native faculty.

We see the perceptive and assimilative capacity of woman
in the smallest incidents of daily life. As W. F. Roscoe
wrote: "A woman sees a thousand things which escape a

as being bound up with woman's physical constitution, and especially
with the important rôle played by the sympathetic nervous system.
"The womanly lack of sense for the abstract cannot be much altered
by education or instruction, because it is rooted in woman's physiological structure." Women, it is added, have a stronger memory than
men for all those ideas, recollections, and experiences that are tinged
with emotion; they participate more warmly in the inner life of the
individual, and possess a better intuitive knowledge of human nature,
as well as more altruism, and more capacity for sympathy, patience, and
self-abnegation. (*Das Weib,* by Oskar Schultze and Max Hirsch (Leipzig,
Curt Kabitsch, 1928).)

man. . . . Mentally she takes in many more impressions in the same time than a man does. A woman will have mastered the minutest details in another woman's dress and noted all the evidence of character in her face before a man, who has been equally occupied in examining her, knows the details of her features."[1] And Mill remarked: "A woman usually sees much more than a man of what is immediately before her."

We must avoid making generalisations which taken too literally will seem crude, but we should not be far from the mark in saying that woman's mentality centres in *the concrete and actual*, either outward or inward; while the masculine mentality, in its typical form, has its roots in the world of *the abstract and rational*. Women are extraordinarily aware of reality in its immediacy, whether this be given in the form of an external object, such as another person, or makes itself felt as a feeling, such as fear, hate, or love. Their mentality, on the other hand, is relatively opaque to the abstract and the ideal, in an intellectual sense. The idealism of many women social reformers and feminists is much more an aspect of emotion than an appreciation of the ideal in an intellectual sense. It would, for example, be inconceivable that a woman could have evolved the philosophy of Plato. As Lecky truly said of women: "Their thinking is chiefly a mode of feeling."

[1] The reader is referred to *Poems and Essays* by William Caldwell Roscoe (edited by R. H. Hutton), which contains an essay entitled *Woman* (written in 1858). This is one of the soundest contributions to the subject of this chapter that we possess in the English language, and all the more interesting because Roscoe, writing in the very early stages of the movement for the higher education of women, foresaw, with prophetic vision, many of the evils which would ensue if this education was based upon wrong views of woman's psychology and functions. Even seventy years ago it was possible for Roscoe to write that women were being bred who think "that if they are not men, it is only by some great injustice which demands instant remedy".

All the leading students of the psychology of sex agree in asserting that the typical woman is nearer than man to nature, to the primitive and the instinctive, and it is just *this closeness to concrete reality* which makes the mind of woman so much more flexible and impressionable than that of man. Professor G. Heymans (see p. 187) writes of woman's power of adapting her mind to "an unlimited multiplicity of different circumstances" and "its marvellous receptivity for the finest shades of reality", as contrasted with the more "precise and rigid" masculine mind, which cannot adapt itself to the particularities of special cases and circumstances, owing to its attachment to fixed rules and mental formulæ.

It must not be forgotten that for countless thousands of years women have been pre-eminently concerned with human affairs, with the management of men and children, and this has bred in women a keenness of insight and a vivid sense of reality in all matters appertaining to personality, character, and social affairs, which places them, in this department of life, on quite a different level from men. Man's absorption throughout the ages in active pursuits, such as hunting, warfare, seafaring, agriculture, and so forth, has distracted his mind from the more intimate and personal side of life, so that he remains greatly inferior to his mate in all the qualities which are naturally developed through a preoccupation with this personal side.[1]

[1] Dr. Charlotte Bühler (see p. 67) has made a special study of the diaries of young people, from a psychological standpoint. She found that the girls' diaries centre in the world of persons, and are taken up with observations of a predominantly human and subjective nature. The chief subjects of comment are friendships, personal thoughts and feelings, and comments on people. The boys' diaries are all alike in showing a main interest in the objective side of life—in ships, railways, inventions of all sorts, historical incidents, games, school affairs, and so on.

That searching critic of modern life, Mr. H. L. Mencken, is of the opinion that women possess "an intelligence so keen that it can penetrate to the hidden truth through the most formidable wrappings of semblance and demeanour", and that they "see at a glance what most men could not see with searchlights and telescopes; they are at grips with the essentials of a problem before men have finished debating its mere externals. They are the supreme realists of the race." "Apparently unobservant", they see "with merciless perspicacity." Yet in spite of all these qualities, it is man and not woman who has given the world the great works of genius, and this Mr. Mencken explains, in typical style, as follows: "Man without a saving touch of the woman in him is too doltish, too naïve and romantic, too easily deluded and lulled to sleep by his imagination, to be anything above a cavalryman, a theologian, or a bank director. And woman, without some trace of that divine innocence which is masculine, is too harshly the realist for those vast projections of the fancy which lie at the heart of what we call genius." Mr. Mencken's *In Defence of Women* is one of the acutest modern contributions to the themes we are discussing. When we have allowed for his whimsical exaggerations, there remains a core of solid truth. Nothing could be better than his exposure of the idea that women will "advance" by participating more largely in what he calls "the masculine bag of tricks"! "A man thinks he is more intelligent than his wife because he can understand . . . the imbecile jargon of the stock market . . . or the minutiæ of some sordid and degrading business or profession." The fact that women, speaking broadly, do not succeed at these sordid tasks is no proof of inferiority. They are brilliantly successful at far more important and difficult tasks, such as managing refractory husbands, rearing children, or smoothing over social difficulties. The woman who makes a success of business or the law is probably a less intelligent woman than her sister who brings up a family on a small income. The force and originality of Mr. Mencken's argument is explicable through his emancipation from the popularly accepted masculine standards. He realises, with the most refreshing clearness, that the traditional occupations of womankind are really more important, as well as more interesting, than the tiresome routine which makes up nine-tenths of the modern man's life. Woman fails, he considers, in occupations demanding technical competence, but she succeeds, for example, in nursing; "for that profession requires ingenuity, quick comprehension, courage in the face of novel and disconcerting situations, and, above all, a capacity for penetrating and dominating character". Of special value, too, in Mr. Mencken's work, is the humorous exposure of the idea, so widely prevalent (especially in Anglo-Saxon lands), that women are the idealistic and civilising sex. If by civilisation we mean domestic manners and polite conversation, there may be a measure of truth in this point of view; but it remains a fact that all, or nearly all, the great inspirers of civilisation, in the deeper sense of the term, have been men.

The ideal influences which have been epoch-making for our own European civilisation sprang from the minds of such men as Socrates, Aristotle, St. Thomas Aquinas, the Italian artists of the Renaissance, Luther, Kant, Descartes, Beethoven, and the inspirers of the French Revolution. When Emerson answered the question "What is civilisation?" by saying: "It is the influence of good women", he revealed the narrow New England streak in him and a total lack of understanding for what Europe means by civilisation. We must charitably assume that the sage was in a mood of unguarded sentimentality when he uttered this extraordinary dictum, for we can hardly suppose that he was capable of denying the significance of all the achievements of the master minds of the ages. On p. 508 of vol. iii of that monument of learning and research, *The Mothers*, we find Mr. Robert Briffault, who cannot be accused of any anti-feminine bias, saying: "Those achievements which constitute what, in the best sense, we term civilisation have taken place in societies organised on patriarchal principles; they are for the most part the work of men. Women have had very little share in them. Women are constitutionally deficient in the qualities that mark the masculine intellect." If Emerson had been content to say that when a higher significance is attached to woman's true nature than is now the case we shall see a more humane and more beautiful civilisation than that of the patriarchies of history, he would have been talking sound sense, and not sentiment worthy of a place in a ballad of the "Take me back to Tennessee" order. If we are ever to obtain a true view of woman's psychology and social functions, it is necessary to rise above all that is merely vague and sentimental.

To quote Dr. Arabella Kenealy, woman "remains at core a creature of instinct, not of reason. As a creature of instinct she is invaluable to Life—because Life is moulded upon instinct." The intellectual work of woman unfolds itself within a framework built by man, just as the physical life of man develops within a framework built by woman.

It is as *the custodian of life*—using the phrase in its very widest sense—that woman makes her unique contribution to civilisation.

f. Some Recent Contributions to Sex Psychology

In reviewing the literature of sex psychology, we cannot fail to be impressed by the unanimity which exists between writers of different nationalities and different schools of thought. For example, Professor Heymans shows us that a report on the characteristics and abilities of French women students, prepared by a number of French professors and teachers, gave results which, from a psychological point of view, were almost identical with those obtained from a similar report prepared (wholly independently) in Germany by German professors and teachers. The Englishman, Havelock Ellis; the Dutchman, Heymans; the Germans, Schultze, Lippmann, and Heilbronn; and the Swiss, Klages (to mention only one or two leading names), all come to conclusions which, if not identical, are so similar as to make quite absurd the view that there is no such thing as well-established knowledge on the subject of sex distinction.

The broad outlines of typical sex distinction have been indicated in the foregoing sections. This typical distinction is corroborated, not only by modern observation, but by the opinions expressed throughout history by men and women of all nations, from East to West and North to South. It is supported by the views of that almost infallible observer Aristotle, by the lore of tribes, by our proverbs and saws, by the visions of poets, and by the literary analysis of our novelists.

In modern times it has been expressed with poetic insight by Shakespeare and Goethe, perhaps the two ripest minds of modern Europe. Nothing could exceed the devotion, single-mindedness, realism, and courage of Shakespeare's heroines; but men are the vehicles of his ideas. (In passing, what a curious light the study of Shakespeare throws upon the feminist myth of the suppression of women in former times!)

.   .   .   .   .

In one of the most modern works on sex psychology, that of Professor Heymans, of Groningen (Holland)—obtainable in an excellent German translation entitled *Die Psychologie der Frauen*—we have an analysis of the feminine character and personality which is of great value for all who wish to study seriously the problems touched upon in this chapter —an analysis based, not upon mere opinion or theory, but almost wholly upon an immense series of exact observations carried out mainly upon students and boys and girls, but also, to some extent, upon older persons.

Professor Heymans sent out inquiry papers to fifty-four Dutch schools, containing questions as to character and ability, with special reference to sex. All these papers were filled up quite independently; and yet, in almost every respect, the hundreds of teachers who filled in the answers agree in their estimates of male and female ability. Similar inquiries were conducted, through the medium of trained scientific observers, as to the distinctive mental and emotional characteristics of persons known very closely to them (in all some 2,500 in number). A comparison of the results obtained by this last method agreed closely with the results obtained from the schools, although there was no relationship between the two investigations. It would be inconceivable that such a degree of correspondence could be due to coincidence. Professor Heymans also brings in the results of the above-mentioned French and German analyses, and the results of a very careful investigation of the abilities and characteristics of Dutch students at *all* the Dutch universities. For details the reader is referred to the book itself. In general, it was seen that the girls and young women excelled very markedly in "keenness", quickness of apprehension, patience and application, and rather less markedly in memory. On the other hand, they were left far behind in power of reasoning, the capacity to apply knowledge practically, in originality, in initiative, and in power of abstraction.

In a table summing up the observations upon students (in

particular), we find that the men easily led in the application of knowledge, in originality of thought, depth of special knowledge, love of independent reading (i.e. in reading apart from examination purposes), powers of logic, and abstract thought in general; in critical capacity, in initiative, in love of science, and (rather unexpectedly) in practical dexterity (in experimental work, and so forth). Those qualities in which the girl students exhibited a clearly marked superiority were mainly of a moral order, such as perseverance, application to studies, order, good attendance, patience, conscientiousness, and general "steadiness". In memory and in school knowledge they were also placed above the men, and in "keenness". In some directions, such as originality and power of abstract thought, their inferiority was very marked indeed.

From the French report Professor Heymans quotes a passage, from which I take the following:

"De toutes parts, on célèbre leur application, leur conscience et leur zèle. . . . Mais, en général . . . si elles montrent plus de mémoire et des connaissances plus sérieuses, plus complètes et plus précises que les hommes, en revanche, elles manquent d'indépendance et de profondeur dans la pensée. Elles sont plus recéptives que créatrices. Leurs qualités seraient plutôt négatives."

From the German report, it appears that the qualities in which women students took precedence were diligence, sense of duty, quickness of apprehension, and sharpness of observation. Their greatest deficiencies were in independence, objectivity of thought, logic, power of abstraction, and originality.

It would appear, according to Professor Heymans, that (making a very broad distinction) it is the abstract which appeals to the male and the concrete to the female (in the abstract we include technics); and he quotes Havelock

Ellis: "The masculine preference is for the more remote, the constructive, the useful, the general, and the abstract"; the feminine preference for "the finished product, the ornamental, the individual, and the concrete". The reader will also remember the work of Dr. Bühler, in which this preference was shown to be so apparent in diaries (see p. 183). "The bloodless coldness of abstraction is inwardly repugnant to women, because their emotional needs find no satisfaction in this field", writes Heymans. Further, he quotes from the philosopher Lotze: "The knowledge and will of the man is taken up with the general, that of the woman with the complete whole. . . . Women hate analysis, while they enjoy and admire the finished whole, in its completeness, in its immediate value and beauty." We refer to Lotze's acute observation that women almost invariably take a great interest in making their surroundings (rooms, gardens, clothing, etc.) orderly and beautiful; but with respect to time (keeping of appointments, etc.) are far less exact than men—a fact which is naturally explained by the feminine love of the concrete and their dislike for abstractions, such as time.

As an example of the feminine indifference to analysis we may note the extreme rarity of the little girl who takes her toys to pieces to see how they work, a form of activity which is one of the most typical characteristics of small boys. The girl loves to arrange her toys and to have a personal relationship with them, but she is not at all interested in knowing how they work.

A complete account of Professor Heymans's very systematic and cautious book would take us too far afield. He deals with his subject from every possible point of view, while following a strictly inductive scientific method; and he does not fail to point out the perils of John Stuart Mill's rough-and-ready deductions, whereby Mill postulated a theoretical woman (free from attributes due to environment or education), and then deduced from this hypothetical being what women could or could not do, how they should be educated, etc.—all without any consideration of the actual psychology of woman. Heymans's book represents, indeed, the exact antithesis to Mill's *The Subjection of Women.* The former is purely scientific and impartial; the latter didactic and propagandist, but wholly devoid of any accurate foundation. As Heymans so truly observes, reality is infinitely complex; and the attempt to establish all-too-simple theories of sex equality by crude deduction, while ignoring the observed realities of feminine and masculine nature and behaviour, is to lose ourselves in a sea of error.

The final conclusion of the Dutch psychologist is that woman's most important distinctive quality is her *emotionality*—by which he does not mean sentimentality (which is quite another thing, and more often found in men), but the predominance of instinct and feeling, of the irrational and elemental, in the feminine nature.

One of the most interesting attempts to set forth salient mental sex distinctions we owe to Ludwig Klages, of Zürich, whose works on character-psychology have aroused great interest on the Continent. Klages has for many years made human character, its types and distinctions, his special study, and his opinion on the subject of this chapter is of considerable weight. Amongst masculine qualities he places in the front rank: objectivity and the power of abstraction, the capacity of absorption in impersonal matters (as the drawback to this quality, men are much less realistic than women, and more likely to be the victims of illusion). Practical energy and initiative, too, are more frequently found in the male, but these qualities often degenerate into lack of feeling and restlessness. In width of vision, imagination, and many-sidedness, men are also given first place. In general,

Klages regards the male psychology as being marked by strong differentiation and a lack of inner unity. The man can more easily split up his personality. The woman, on the other hand, is much more a unity. Whatever she does she does with wholeness, and the oneness of her nature makes it much more difficult for her to detach herself from subjective impulses. Women are more closely bound up with nature and all that is elementary, and less liable to self-deception (the drawback to these qualities being the dependence of women upon the personal side of life and their lack of objectivity). In common with the other authorities we have quoted, Klages lays weight on woman's sense of concrete reality and comparative immunity from illusion, and on her intuitive faculty (accompanied often by opacity to reason). Woman's patience, devotion, and strong sense of pity, and her natural warmth of feeling are amongst the other points in Klages's list of feminine attributes. For our study it is of significance that one who has approached the whole problem of sex distinction from a fresh standpoint, quite uninfluenced by what others may have said, relying wholly on his own personal observations, should have thus reaffirmed the broad lines of distinction which have been placed before the reader of this chapter.

A very interesting corroboration of the above lines of distinction between the sexes is to be found in a study of recent feminist books and articles written by women. Although most of the authoresses in question do not admit the existence of typical mental sex differences, their own writings are a good example of the reality of such differences. These works show, almost without exception, a high intuitive sense (accompanied by a lack of exactitude), strong emotionality, a violent one-sidedness of outlook (lack of objectivity), imagination and vision (with a poor logical analysis), and an intense dislike for abstraction (as evidenced, for example, in the determination to avoid generalisations as to sex distinctions). All these are very typical feminine qualities. On the other hand, the classical example of a book on the same topic written by a man—John Stuart Mill's *Subjection of Women*—shows an utterly different type of mentality. It is reasoned, abstract to a defect, lacking in intuition and imagination, and full of logic (based upon incorrect premises!).

N

CHAPTER VIII

WOMAN AND SOCIETY

"If woman's nature were really the same as that of man, it would be a superfluity, a mere tautology . . . If women acquire the view that sex difference is only physical, and that mentally and spiritually they are of the same nature as men, and if they act on this assumption (thus giving life a one-sidedly masculine form), then our civilisation will sooner or later sink into utter confusion and chaos."—RABINDRANATH TAGORE.

HAVING seen, in the foregoing chapter, that the question of sex distinction is capable of receiving a well-defined answer, it remains to consider how far we can make use of our knowledge in the organisation of society.

Do we intend to continue the present chaotic and utterly unpsychological system by which a distinction deeply rooted in reality is almost wholly ignored? Or do we propose to make a sincere effort to train men and women along (broadly speaking) the lines of their congenital capacities and aptitudes, so that, as far as is humanly possible, square pegs shall not be put into round holes?

It may be true that we cannot draw a clear line between work that is suitable for men and work that is suitable for women. We must endeavour to leave room for the free play of ability wherever it can be found. But it is equally true that the vast majority of women do differ fundamentally from men in their potentialities. If this is not adequately realised to-day, it is largely because the feminine side of life is so undervalued and underdeveloped that the normal girl scarcely gets a chance of showing her inherent powers. From an early age she is forced into masculine grooves. But once let women be educated and occupied along lines thoroughly adapted to their innate abilities, and we shall be able to enrich our civilisation through the utilisation of aspects of reality now increasingly neglected.

It is generally admitted that a chief and growing danger of our present-day civilisation is the mechanisation of life. The human and personal side of life is being more and more restricted. We tend to become typified along narrow lines of specialisation. Woman is the *universalist*, the natural enemy of one-sided specialisation such as now threatens us. She is the heaven-sent guardian of the springs of personal and individual life. All her natural and instinctive characteristics such as emotionality (in the sense we have explained) intuition, sympathy, practicality, adaptability, catholicity o tastes, personal devotion, patience, and profound interest in individuals, are precisely those required for the development and intensification of personal life. How all-important it must therefore be that woman in the mass should not suffer conquest by the machine of technics and industry, but that these qualities (rarely found in the opposite sex in the same degree) should be *systematically cultivated* and mobilised in the service of a civilisation which so urgently needs them. But in order to do this we must break away from our present-day educational and social ideals and place a much stronger emphasis upon the fundamental idea of human bi-polarity. In preceding sections I have sought to show that confusion follows when we seek to ignore this vital principle. The present chapter is an attempt to outline the relationship of Woman to Society, as it appears from the standpoint of bi-polarity and in the light of the view of sex psychology unfolded above.

a. Woman's Positive Task

One of the chief errors introduced into our social life by the equalitarian-utilitarian school of thinkers was the doctrine that, outside the purely functional field, there is nothing of importance to differentiate woman's work from man's work. This attitude follows naturally from their sexless philosophy.

Hence the plea of Olive Schreiner and other spokeswomen of the feminist party for woman's right of entry into every branch of economic and cultural life:

"From the judge's seat to the legislator's chair, from the statesman's closet to the merchant's office, from the chemist's laboratory to the astronomer's tower, there is no post or form of toil for which it is not our intention to attempt to fit ourselves."

In this oft-quoted passage, from *Woman and Labour*, which admirably expresses the spirit of the modern Woman's Movement, we see the implication of a negative life-outlook —woman is *to fit herself to man's world*; she is not to build up a new world, suited to her own needs and enabling her to better the civilisation of to-day by creating richer and more human relationships than those which have grown up under the mechanical life-construction. Save as an economic necessity, there is not the slightest need for women to be astronomers or chemists. It is most improbable that they will advance these sciences faster than they would be advanced by men. On the other hand, when we consider the factories, the offices, the slums of to-day, the mass of human wreckage in our cities, and the appalling physical and moral degradation of large sections of population in the modern world, we see an immeasurable field of opportunity, where women, by virtue of their own inherent qualities, can do a work which is indispensable. Here it is they alone who can save civilisation. When we remember that there are hundreds of thousands of neglected and half-starved children in our great centres of population, it is clear what a wide field is still open for redemptive human activity of a kind specially congenial to women.[1]

---

[1] Consider, for example, the magnificent work amongst poor children that has been done at Deptford by Rachel and Margaret McMillan. If this kind of redemptive and educational work were to be expanded

It may, of course, be said that women will enter into both fields. But it is my contention that the doing of the one thing tends to prevent the other being done. The entry of enormous masses of women into our factories, workshops, and business houses withdraws them from other fields of work in which far more essential service might have been rendered. One of the main causes for the neglect of children and adolescent young folk lies in the absorption of womanly attention elsewhere. A police court missionary said recently, referring to his experiences amongst youthful prostitutes: "These girls would not be on the street at all if their mothers had looked after them properly." It would be interesting to know what proportion of the daughters of careful and conscientious mothers have joined the host of street-walkers—probably not one in ten thousand. (In the *Revolt of Youth* (see p. 221) the author states that the widespread moral laxity which he so vividly describes is due mainly to the decay of home-life.) Again, in many of the centres where women participate largely in industry we find an appalling neglect of child-life and widespread moral degeneration.

In opposition to the standpoint represented in the above quotation from Olive Schreiner, I maintain that woman *as woman* has an immeasurable sphere of work inside *and outside* the home, a sphere in which she can exert, for the benefit of the community, all her most natural qualities. We are now slowly emerging from the period of mechanical and technical

more than a hundredfold, its beneficial effect would be beyond all calculation, and it would employ a large number of women in a manner ideally suitable to their deepest inward needs. Is it not a thousand pities that the desire of the modern girl for a larger sphere of activity should not be gratified along such lines, thus enriching the future of the nation, rather than in the way of actually destroying our domestic life through a frenzied competition with men in the commercial field? It is officially estimated that about 1,000,000 children in England and Wales are below a (not very high) normal standard of physique and mentality.

civilisation which dominated the nineteenth century. We are beginning to perceive that the mere development of science and its application to life cannot create for us human and fruitful conditions of life. We know now that we need a new culture of the spiritual and personal side of existence. It is just exactly here, in the development of this new culture, that we need the help of women. The more women sink themselves in the life of the factory and the office, the less they can aid us where their assistance is *vital*, because irreplaceable.

Here again we see that the feminists have been betrayed by their shallow rationalist philosophy. It is the lack of a deep, *positive* conception of womanhood which leads them to underrate all that woman, as a being other than man, can do for the community, and to overvalue, correspondingly, her work as a chemist, an astronomer, or what not. We have chemists enough. What we need is a new influence helping us to overcome the narrow, mechanical over-masculinised culture of to-day and to build up a richer, deeper, and more highly individualised type of life.

The next move in the advance of our civilisation must be a campaign against the mechanisation of life, the typification of all that is around us and within us. Not only our motor cars, our houses, our furniture, and our clothes are typified, but our ideas and our ideals. We are confronted by the possibility of a wilderness of Babbitts, of a horrible, soulless, monotonous, factory and Ford-made existence, which will result in the decay of all the ripest fruits of Western civilisation.

The peril of equalitarian feminism, of the usual type, is that it entirely fails to realise either the existence of this danger or the special powers which women possess for counteracting it. An urgent task of the present is to mobilise women for the war against the typification and de-personalisation of life.

In order to do this it is necessary to create the right ideology. If we accept the current philosophy of feminism, we cannot enlist this army at all. Our recruits will disappear into the ranks of the enemy. If our schools and training institutions are busily engaged in training young women to be co-workers with men in the machine which is reducing us all to cogs and rivets, they cannot at the same time be helping to fit out an army of women whose aim it shall be to wage war against the machine.

The main current of modern life sweeps our young womanhood with it into a vast mechanism of soulless, impersonal relationships. As we have seen in the early chapters of this book, the modern educational system has allowed itself, most deplorably, to become to a large extent a feeding-pipe for this machine. It is necessary to rouse opinion to a realisation of the situation, and to raise a new standard around which the forces making for our emancipation from a stereotyped form of existence can group themselves.

Many readers will perhaps follow this line of thought with more or less sympathy, but will all the while feel that, given the existing situation, there is no alternative to the entry of large masses of women into the machine. They will argue that it is all very well to open up here and there opportunities for women to pursue callings more in harmony with their psychology, but that these will be too limited in their scope to be able to embrace more than a very small proportion of the women who now wish, or are compelled, to work outside the home.

I admit quite frankly that this is a weighty objection. It would be foolish to minimise the difficulties and perplexities of the position. It is our fate to find ourselves absorbed in a world-wide process of transition. We live in a period in between the decaying patriarchal order, with its narrow field of work for women, and a period yet to come, when this field will be widened, while yet retaining something that is distinctive. During this transition, women have not seen any better possibility than that of submitting themselves to the tyranny of the mechanical social order established by men.[1]

It must, however, make an immense difference whether we perceive the situation to be what it is or whether we deceive ourselves with the false idea that women, having no distinctive personality, can quite happily submerge themselves in the machinery of the technical age. It is one thing to submit reluctantly to an evil, knowing that it *is* an evil, while seeking a way out, and quite another to hold a false ideal leading us to regard the evil as a blessing.

.   .   .   .   .

In an immediate practical sense we may try to make the most of all those beginnings which promise to lead in the right direction, such as the elevation of domestic work, nursing, and child-education to the rank of dignified occupa-

[1] A glimpse at the cold realities of life in our great cities will show us to what a pass this submission has brought women. The following is an accurate account of the conditions of life in one of the London stores where young women are employed: In a large hostel eighty girls live together, three in each bedroom, the average wage being about £2 per week. From this, 26s. is deducted for board and insurance, leaving 14s. to pay for clothes, boots and shoes, laundry, holidays, amusements, etc. The girls must be well dressed and always polite and cheerful, or they are liable to instant dismissal. The hours are from about nine till six-thirty. The life is one of unutterable monotony. There is no social life; the girls do not even possess a social room in the hostel, which consists solely of bedrooms; and the worst day in the week is felt to be Sunday, save for those who have special friends or connections in London. Small wonder that no small proportion of these girls find that the only way open to them of bringing some "life" into the drab round of their existence is by way of the "kind young gentlemen" whom they meet as they stroll along the streets in their couple of hours of daily release from prison. Such are the *real* results of the "emancipation" of women as we see it in operation around us.

tions, *scientifically studied, properly paid, and socially valued*; and, further, the expansion of fields of work well suited to woman's psychology (such as art-handicrafts, house decoration, architecture, gardening, and various lines of social work as yet insufficiently developed). To this topic we return shortly in greater detail.

Of primary importance at the present moment is the conflict in the world of ideas and ideals. A vast deal more could be done than is done to expand the scope of woman's characteristic activities if this *were definitely our purpose*. The main difficulty is the wide influence exerted by the philosophy of life which regards the evil of masculinisation as a blessing and an aim desirable in itself.

b. THE BATTLE OF IDEAS

While there can be no room for doubt as to the ultimate victory of this positive, characteristic feminism, founded as it is upon the essential bi-polarity of the human species and answering as it does to the teachings of biology and psychology, it is well to see clearly the nature and extent of the difficulties which must be overcome before the conflict is decided.

In common with all root problems, *the problem of woman's true place in the social system is linked up with our fundamental life-philosophy*. If life be regarded as a mechanical affair, a struggle between separate units not organically related to one another, we shall tend to regard woman as an isolated unit; and, without going further into the question of her inner nature, it will seem only right and just that she should claim the same position in the system as that occupied by the mass of male units. But if we see life as a whole, in which every part is linked by an inner purpose to every other part, all working together with a single purpose—in other words, if our standpoint is that of *immanence* if we look at life from within and not from without—we shall tend to see in the division of sex a distinction which must have an ultimate significance. If we believe that there is a purpose immanent in Nature, it follows that all the distinctions inherent in Nature will have some part to play within the scheme of the whole. We shall aim at finding out exactly what these distinctions are, and then helping them to their fullest development in the service of the whole.

What Benjamin Kidd called the "self-assertive rationalism of the individual" is the typical tendency of the age, and is rooted in the all-too-masculine life of the nineteenth century. The opposed tendency, anabolic or life-creating, is required to hold in balance the self-assertive spirit and to subordinate the latter to the needs of the race. The born cultivators of the creative spirit, in its application to all social questions, are the women of the community. The conquest of the Woman's Movement, at any rate in the Anglo-Saxon countries, by the rationalist spirit results, in practice, in the Movement being diverted from its true path. It has now ceased to hold the balance which should keep the social life of the community healthy. On the one hand, masculine reason and self-assertion, intellectual creation and scientific organisation; on the other, feminine feeling and intuition, self-surrender in the interest of the race, life-creation, and personal and family life.

The adoption by so many women of the whole masculine life-outlook, system of values and "bag of tricks", as Mr. Mencken calls it, would (if Nature were not after all rather too strong) threaten to upset altogether the natural bi-polarity of human society. As it is, the balance is not wholly destroyed, but receives a disastrous tilt towards the individualistic self-assertive side, with the result that the interests of the race are insufficiently safeguarded. The withdrawal of practical life from religious influence has allowed our social system to fall under the influence of utilitarianism, which tends to regard women as so much material for the economic machine and nothing more. The separation between science and religion has led to the whole of Nature (including all that is related to sex) being relegated to a watertight compartment, where it exists without having any points of contact with the spiritual life. Religion, in its turn, has drawn away from Nature, so that the modern man sees no hidden meaning in the life of Nature or in sex. Religious life has become transcendental, and the life of Nature, which under the influence of a religion of immanence is illumined with purpose, has lost its inward significance in our minds. It thus seems easy to mould society along the lines of the equalitarian-utilitarians and abolish sex distinction as a basic social principle. That this denial of the true inwardness of the problem is bound to lead us into social morasses of every description is certain. In order to climb out of the boggy country in which we are straying we must find some solid ground of first principles, such as I have sought to sketch in the preceding chapter.

.   .   .   .   .

On page 124 of *Woman and Labour*, the superficial materialistic philosophy which has hindered the Feminist Movement from the days of the ill-starred Mary Wollstonecraft onwards, pops its head out of the bag, and we see it face to face. Here Olive Schreiner explains that the approaching period will be a time of strain and difficulty, when "Mankind seeks rapidly to adjust moral ideals and social relationships . . . to the new and continually unfolding material conditions." *Here we see clearly that moral ideals are to be adapted to the material conditions.* This is a fatalistic and non-moral attitude towards life which implicitly denies the power of the human will to mould our social life. It is precisely on a par with the general doctrine of the feminists that women must perforce adjust themselves to the masculine world, as if they were creatures without any will or purpose of their own. In each case the given material conditions are regarded as totally inevitable and unalterable. But, unless we entirely disbelieve in the human spirit as a creative force, we are not at all bound to accept the conditions around us and the tendencies of modern "progress" as inescapable realities. We can do something to mould our own destiny. This underlying weakness is peculiarly evident in the attitude of Olive Schreiner and most other feminists towards home and family life, as well as in their passive acceptance of industrialism and the mechanisation of life.

Again and again we read of the decay of the family, the reduction in the importance and interest of home duties, the decline in the number of women who marry, and so forth, as if all these things were imposed upon us by some process over which we had absolutely no control. But it is we ourselves who are mainly responsible for all these developments. *If women were determined to save the family, it would not decay;* and we have seen in this chapter and in an earlier one that the decline of woman's marriage opportunity is a matter which has nothing inevitable about it. What is the matter with modern society is that our vast social mechanism has got out of control. There is to-day an extraordinary dearth of organising ability and of personalities who stand sufficiently above the turmoil of separate interests to take a wide and objective view of social life. Mr. G. K. Chesterton has protested (in an article in *Time and Tide*, December 1926) against "the making of an inhuman fate out of something that depends entirely on a human will", and in this article, with his customary penetration, he fixes on the passive and fatalistic acceptance of de-humanising conditions as the basic weakness of the women's Emancipation Movement.

If women as a body were to throw themselves into the struggle against the mechanisation and de-spiritualisation of life and insist on the importance of those aspects of life in which women have always naturally believed, they might do a vast deal to help in the reorganisation of civilisation.

Even the much despised domestic work itself might be made much more interesting than is now the case. A feminist writer says: "The working woman of to-day goes out and buys her dinner in tins. She no longer takes a personal interest in the preparation of meals", and from this observation the moral is drawn, of course, that regular outside work must be given to the poor creature to make up for her lack of interest! But nobody compels her to go out and buy tinned things! If she had any desire to do so, there is no power in the world to prevent her taking a keen interest in preparing food which would probably be both cheaper and healthier than the tinned things. Moreover, there is not the slightest reason to believe that the work in some tailor's shop or factory to which the feminist beckons the bored housewife would be any more interesting than intelligent domestic work—which possesses at any rate the merit of variety.

In the same article, Mr. Chesterton inveighs against the doctrine of "the coming of the small family", as if this were a decree of fate against which it were hopeless to rebel, although it is well enough known that many families are small solely through the will of the parents concerned, and in a very large proportion of these cases they are not acting under any immediate economic compulsion. In the various articles by protagonists of the feminist standpoint which appeared at about the same time as Mr. Chesterton's and in the same periodical, great play was made with the idea that the decline in the size of families made it "inevitable" that the modern educated married woman should seek professional work outside the home. It did not seem to have occurred to any of these people that it might be well worth while to encourage larger families in these circles (in which the birth-rate is by general admission much too low); and that these women would be far more usefully employed in helping to save the best English stocks from decline than in swelling the array of women working in competition with men.

.   .   .   .   .

It is primarily *our false moral values* which cause us to think that women are on the road towards emancipation when they feed their children on tinned things and seek for "development" outside the home; or when the women of the educated classes are urged by feminist leaders to enter into masculine occupations of every kind rather than to concentrate upon making their own homes more interesting and more racially valuable. Mrs. Colquhoun puts the matter very well: "It is . . . a question of artificial standards. There is nothing intrinsically finer about one kind of work than about another. The only true criterion is the standard of the work itself and its usefulness to the community. We have set up a feminine scale of values, with a female professor at the top and a kitchen wench at the bottom; but it is quite an arbitrary scale. The world wants both—the kitchen wench, probably, even more than the professor. Let us be honest, therefore, and acknowledge that part, at all events, of the compulsion which drives women into the open labour market is not economic necessity, but their own tastes, habits, and theory of gentility." (*The Vocation of Woman*, chap. vii.)

In other words, the whole problem of the position of

woman in society is bound up with our standards of values, and is in reality far less of an economic question than is supposed by most modern writers. As Havelock Ellis so forcibly points out (see *Sex in Relation to Society*), the weak spot in Anglo-Saxon civilisation is the lack of racial feeling, the over-emphasis of all that is individual and the corresponding undervaluation of all those tasks which are connected with the maintenance of the race (domestic work, maternity, nursing, and so on).

These departments of work are not in themselves less interesting than the more masculine departments, such as business or factory work. Nothing, as a matter of fact, could be more ridiculous than the idea that the office is a paradise of liberty and the home a sort of gilded cage. Most office work is appallingly monotonous and almost entirely devoid of human interest. Home work is full of variety, and *if done with inspiration* abounds in educational opportunities. The really capable and intelligent housewife must be a cook, a dressmaker, a nurse, a chemist, a gardener, a kindergarten teacher, a secretary, and two or three other things, all in one. The office worker is usually nothing but a typist or a short-hand-writer, doing the same work over and over again.

The next step forward in the working out of a new synthesis must be our emancipation from a sexless utilitarianism which makes nothing of racial matters, and passes without a thought over the profound teleological significance of human bi-polarity. Thus overcoming false and superficial ideas, we might hope to evolve a new ideology of the problem, envisaging woman as man's complement and co-worker, dedicated first and foremost to the maintenance and elaboration of the human and personal side of civilisation. Once grounded in a definite philosophy of woman's life and work, we could at least make an attempt to bring some order into the chaos of modern individualism.

The true point of view has been most happily put by Dr. Arabella Kenealy in her very suggestive book *Feminism and Sex Extinction*. In the foreword she insists that progress results from "an opposite trend, in inherence and development, of the two sexes, as regards Life and characteristics, aptitude and avocation. The progressive differentiations and specialisations of vital processes and living forms, whereby human character and faculty have been increasingly advanced to higher powers, reach their most admirable culmination in the complex division of Humanity into two genders, each of which is enabled by way of such complex specialisation to promote, to intensify, and to dignify its own allotted order of qualities. . . . Nature, marvellously prescient in all her processes, has provided that the sexes, by being constituted wholly different in body, brain, and bent, do not normally come into rivalry and antagonism in the fulfilment of their respective life-rôles. Their faculties and functions, being complementary and supplementary (and obviously best applied, therefore, in different departments of Life and of Labour), men and women are naturally dependent upon one another in every human relation, a dispensation which engenders reciprocal trust, affection, and comradeship."

c. THE SOCIAL IDEAL

Bearing in mind the central importance of the conflict in the world of ideas, we shall not allow ourselves to be led astray by the oft-repeated argument that the entry of women into every sort of occupation and career is solely an economic problem, that the present situation is conditioned by the large excess of women over men, by the loss of manhood in the war, and so on. We have already seen in Chapter IV that the enormous proportion of unmarried women (especially in the educated classes) is the result, not mainly of a shortage of men, but of the inability or unwillingness of the existing men (or their mates) to marry—a state of things which, in its turn, is a result, to no small extent, of the intense competition of women in the economic field. We live in an age in which all the factors making for family life are systematically discouraged in favour of those encouraging individual independence. Without any alteration in the relative proportion of men to women, the entire situation would be revolutionised if half (or even one-third) of the unmarried men between the ages of twenty and fifty were enabled to marry, if most married women workers ceased to work outside their homes, and if some considerable proportion of the women now doing men's work were taken out of their present occupations and employed in work that would not have employed men. In this fashion, at the very least one million vacant situations would be created (in England and Wales). These would absorb the unemployed, who in their turn would spend money, stimulate trade, and create still more employment. We should then have started a "virtuous circle", the beneficial results of which would be incalculable.

In the ideal state (as seen from the standpoint of the organic and bi-polar view of society) conditions might be envisaged (speaking quite roughly) as follows: granted that the proportion of men to women was the same as that now existing in England—100 to 110 (in round numbers)—and assuming that some 80 per cent. of the men were married (not at all too high a figure), we should then have thirty women and girls requiring work out of a group of 210 adults (if no married women, or only a very small proportion, worked outside the home). If we assume that two-thirds of these were taken up in specifically women's work (such as nursing, kindergarten work, dressmaking, domestic work, women's shops, and so on), there would remain no more than ten women, out of the total of 210 adults, for whom permanent work would have to be found which in any way competed with men's work. This would not constitute any problem at all, since these ten would consist of the specially gifted women who definitely wished to pursue careers as (for example) doctors, artists, lawyers, architects, or inspectors, and whose work is of high value to the community (if they are really gifted women, and not such as are thrust into these occupations because they do not know what else to do!).[1] If fewer women wished to marry, well and good; it would not be at all difficult for the community to find work for more than this 10 per 210 if needful. In such a state there would be no unemployment due to the competition of women, and every woman who wanted to found a home would have a fair chance to do so. At the same time there would be adequate scope for women in the professions, since it is unlikely that the proportion of women who wish to devote themselves *permanently* to a professional career really exceeds the above proportion of some 5 per cent.

This imaginary social order is sketched as an indication of what might be possible if we seriously endeavoured to set aside some of the present evils. I am, of course, aware that it could not be realised in the England of to-day, if only for the reason that the proportion of modern English people who desire to see women engaged in every sort of competitive work rather than see them building up the home-life of the

[1] It may, of course, be objected that some women would be desirous of pursuing careers of this kind side by side with marriage. Under such a social system as I suggest this would not be impossible, and in this way the above figures of women needing employment would be to a slight extent increased; but the number of women falling under this category is, however, in all probability very small. In giving a purely tentative outline, such as is here attempted, it is not practicable to include every aspect of the problem. I am seeking, primarily, to make it clear that a systematic building-up of the home-life of the nation along the above lines would greatly reduce the existing unhealthy sex competition.

nation is so large that it can be relied upon to sabotage every attempt made to remedy the present evils of unemployment, the decay of home-life, and so forth. The idea is here thrown out in order to show the reader what we *could* do, if we wanted to do it, and, especially, to make it clear that the non-marriage and competitive employment of so many women to-day has practically nothing to do with the small excess of women over men, but is due almost wholly to our own lack of organising ability in social matters.

The advantages of the above social ideal are so obvious and manifold that it is scarcely needful for me to say anything about them. In the first place, 80 women out of 110 are married, in place of about 30 per cent. amongst the highly-educated type of woman in modern England (or a higher proportion, some 50 to 70, in the lower classes). Since most feminists themselves admit that marriage is desirable for the normal woman (although they utterly fail to perceive that their own policy of flooding the market with women has lowered woman's marriage chances more than anything else!), this point must be allowed to carry its full weight. As a corollary to this we must reckon with an improvement in general morality. It is a capital error to overlook the fact that sexual morality has been most adversely affected by the presence in our midst of an immense body of unmarried young people, many of whom have imbibed doctrines of individual freedom which they are ready to apply not in any ideal sense, but purely as an excuse for licence.

In the second place, with a higher marriage-rate there would be a great diminution in the proportion of women in the labour market. This would remedy unemployment by throwing open to unemployed men a large number of places formerly held by women. Supposing that by waving some magic wand it were possible to bring about in the England of to-day such social conditions as I have outlined above, we should have done a vast deal to solve the problem of unemployment. It is not, of course, possible to compel people to marry, but it is certain that much of the celibacy of to-day is due to the vicious circle I have described elsewhere; and that if we could start the stream of social tendency flowing towards the home and not away from it, much could be done to reduce the number of unmarried men under fifty years of age, and parallel therewith to remove a large mass of women from competitive employment. Without at the moment entering into details of how this might be attempted, let us note that in this way we should be taking a step of immense significance in the right direction (the proportion of unmarried men between the ages of twenty and fifty is so large, that if less than one-third of them were to marry they would absorb some three-quarters of a million women).

It is, of course, clear that such reforms as are here suggested could not be carried through in a modern State, such as England or Germany, without deep-going alterations of social method. In particular, a much larger degree of social control of the economic machine would be needful. Such a control would need to be directed *consciously* towards the building up of the racial life of the nation. It would be impossible to carry these reforms through, for example, unless the industries now employing underpaid female labour were reorganised so as to support men paid family wages.

Let us not forget, however, that one of the main obstacles to the payment of higher wages at present is the vast burden imposed upon the community by the unemployed; and it is clear that a large step towards ameliorating unemployment would have been taken were we able to remove a million or more women from the labour market.

My object in depicting an unreal, and probably quite

unattainable, state of social life is to throw up in more vivid contrast the stupidity of the present condition of things. If we consider our problems from a national standpoint and not from the standpoint of individualism, we see at once what injury is inflicted upon the community by the employment of millions of women, most of them young, while we have in our midst an immense army of unemployed men, no small proportion of whom are either married or old enough to get married and found families, were they in employment. An employed woman does not found a family and keep a husband (save, of course, in certain exceptional cases). But the average employed man provides for a wife, and thereby in two directions simultaneously promotes employment: first, by withdrawing a woman from the labour market and opening up a spare "job", and secondly by spending money on the needs of his family, and thereby creating an enlarged demand for goods. The young woman worker, on the other hand, not only (very possibly) keeps a man out of work, but spends an inordinately large proportion of her wages on all sorts of small personal luxuries, with the result that her spending is not, in the long run, of advantage to the national economy.[1]

[1] Professor Wieth-Knudsen, in his book on *Feminism*, has drawn public attention to the economic injury done to a community through the luxury expenditure of young women workers, who spend, for the most part on silk stockings, fancy goods, confectionery, theatres, cinemas, etc., rather than on goods which benefit trade (since luxury expenditure is, in the long run, bad for trade). The Danish economist made a study of conditions in Copenhagen, and found that the women workers of that city are mostly young, and that they nearly all spend the greater part of their income, after paying for bare board and lodging, on luxuries, with results injurious to the economic position of Denmark (especially in the sense that the trade balance is adversely affected).

Another chapter in this story is the immense expenditure of women on cosmetics. This has grown so rapidly that it has now become one of the largest items of national expenditure. Speaking at Indianapolis in February 1928, the American Secretary of State for the Navy stated

If, in addition, as supposed in our imaginary State, married women did not work—save in quite exceptional cases—outside the home, another large army of workers would be withdrawn from the market, thus still further enlarging the demand for labour.

In short, in this society we should have removed some of the principal causes of unemployment and of demoralisation due to it. At the same time the average girl would enjoy an immensely improved chance of marriage, children would be better cared for (since it must be admitted that the employment of mothers outside the home is bad for the children), and much would have been done to create healthier moral conditions throughout the community.

If I am correct in assuming that only a small proportion of women desire a *life* career in some quasi-masculine profession, it could not even be urged against this ideal of society that it hindered the development of the more independent type of woman. She would be better off than she is under present conditions, since the better marriage opportunities of the average girl would leave the field clearer for those who did not wish to marry, but desired to be doctors, architects, lawyers, engineers, politicians, chemists, or what not (since I do not suggest that any careers should be forcibly debarred to women). The worst enemy of the serious woman worker is the dilettante of her own sex.

I am under no illusions as to the practicability of such a society in the modern world. In England the individualistic

that whereas his Department proposed to spend about 150 million pounds on the Navy, the *annual* expenditure of the American people on sweets was about the same sum, and on cosmetics round about 300 million pounds (not dollars). If this fantastic sum were to be reduced by only one-half, the money saved would suffice to re-house nearly the whole of the slum population of New York, or to provide proper medical care and fresh-air treatment for practically all the poor sick children in the United States.

tendency is far too strong to permit of the advanced degree of social control which could alone realise such an organisation. It is scarcely possible, for example, to imagine an English Government prohibiting the employment of married women in industry, although the beneficial consequences of such a step would be of far-reaching significance. It is both the strength and the weakness of England that the sense of personal freedom is strong enough to render any realisation of racial aims through governmental action almost out of the question. If the freedom of the Englishman makes him the greatest of pioneers, there is also the danger that this same sense of freedom, degenerating into anti-social individualism, may create and maintain conditions which render very difficult any purposeful reorganisation of national life.

In addition to this general feeling for freedom, we have to reckon with the special opposition of the feminists to every sort of movement which in any way recognises that women have a function in the State other than that of men. Some even go so far as to oppose legislation which aims at protecting women from the hygienic dangers of different pursuits by legislative means. There is no reason to suppose that this opposition would be in any way modified by the fact that the establishment of conditions approximating to those described would benefit women even more than it would benefit men. For it is true, in spite of all that may be said by the more embittered type of feminist, that the home is the best field of work for the normal woman, and that a policy which was designed to build up the home-life of the nation would in the long run do more to solve the "Woman Question" than any opening of doors into masculine areas of activity could ever do.

As we have already seen, with sufficient clearness, in earlier sections of this study, English feminism reflects, in an exaggerated form, the fundamental individualism of the nation. It is rooted in a view of life which regards the self-development of the individual as the main object of civilisation, even when this development takes place along lines which are injurious to the race. Yet, with the break-up of the philosophy which lies behind this individualism, it is every day becoming more obvious that *the family is the real social unit* ; and nothing could be more valuable than a re-orientation of the Woman's Movement about the idea of the family and the race. As a slogan for such a positive feminism I would suggest:

Save the children; save the family; save the race!

This would give the Movement a basis much more in harmony with the real psychology of woman. As I have sought to illustrate, such a re-orientation, however difficult or painful it might be to bring about (given the existing conditions), would in course of time lead to a type of social life much more favourable to woman's interests than that in which we are now living.

d. Feminism and Monogamy

The reply made by different writers representing the Woman's Movement to the foregoing line of argument throws a rather painful light upon the lack of unity to which we have more than once referred.

On the one hand it is said: "But it is precisely we who are fighting for the family. Look at Mrs. Butler's social purity work! Look at Olive Schreiner's noble plea for a true monogamy!"

On the other they cry: "The family is a patriarchal institution. It is founded upon the idea of private property in women and children. Away with this relic of woman's slavery! We herald in the new era of emancipated woman, bestowing herself freely."

Now which of these voices is the authentic voice of the Woman's Movement? That is the question.

The truth is that in these fundamentals the Movement has not yet found itself. But this leaves the general public in the position of not really knowing in the least what use women will make of their power.

It may be argued that the two tendencies will more or less neutralise each other, and that therefore no revolutionary moral changes are to be feared. But in that case what purpose is served by the Movement? This amounts to a confession that the great moral aims which have always been put forward on behalf of women's emancipation will never be fulfilled.

The situation would be clearer if the right wing of the Movement had definitely repudiated the left wing, as the Labour Party leaders have been compelled to rid themselves of their compromising associations with Communism. But, on the contrary, the Movement (or the "Cause") is continually spoken of as a homogeneous whole. We read articles, for example, about the progress of the Woman's Movement in China, and this progress is hailed with delight by all sections of feminists in the English Press. But on studying the matter more closely, we find that it is the Russian feminists, with their programme of free-love, voluntary abortion, and divorce-while-you-wait, who are spreading their ideas in China.

Are our right-wing feminists in England (members, many of them, of Christian Churches) really delighted about the propagation of free-love ideas in China?

There must, after all, be some limit to the possibilities of compromise, even in England. Co-operation is absurd between those who are fighting to destroy monogamy and those who are pledged to defend it. At present all is confusion. But when public sympathy is enlisted for the Woman's Movement, the public has a right to know whether the family is to be abolished or whether it is to be built up.

It is a truism to say that revolutionary movements are governed from the left. It is no exception, therefore, to an established rule when we see in the feminist ranks a gradual drift toward the left. Moreover, for this there is a logical reason.

"For a number of generations the democratic process ruling the world has meant nothing but release, enfranchisement for freedom, the breaking down of controls and restraints and obstacles. There has been a world-wide detachment of individuals from codes and controls, subjugations and responsibilities, functions and duties. I suggest that this process of dissolution is at an end, and that mankind is faced—is challenged—by the need for reorganisation and re-orientation, political and social and intellectual, quite beyond the power of the negligent common voter and his politicians and the happy-go-lucky education and literature on which our minds are fed."

These words, spoken by Mr. H. G. Wells at the Sorbonne on March 15, 1927, provide the key to a correct interpretation of the present-day situation.

The Woman's Movement of to-day is one of the democratic releases to which Mr. Wells refers. Its one idea has been and is *emancipation*. It has stood overwhelmingly under the influence of tendencies which were purely solvent.

As we have seen again and again in the foregoing pages, the fatal weakness of the modern emancipationist's life-outlook is the "detachment of individuals" from "responsibilities, functions, and duties". The girl of to-day is thus left suspended in mid-air, enjoying "freedom". Her leaders —those to whom she looks for inspiration and suggestion (and how pathetic is the suggestibility of the average adolescent girl!)—have failed to provide her with positive life-aims *organically related to her aptitudes and functions.*

It is indeed true that the process of dissolution, of the breaking down of obstacles and restraints, is not the sole tendency in the complex social life of to-day.

Modern life has produced new syntheses, nuclei of crystallisation. For example, science is a vast complex of interrelated facts that is continually growing, and ramifying into new and more wonderful branches. Further, industry has recently given rise to more and more solid amalgamations, which give humanity new points of contact and new loyalties. A large present-day "combine" may command the allegiance, directly and indirectly, of a million or more men and women. Nationalism is a third synthetic influence of immense power (in present-day Italy, for example). But the important point for us is that none of these synthetic tendencies has any relation whatever to woman *as woman.* They are all of them the product of forms and modes of life that are masculine.

On the other hand, the cultural nuclei of the world of the pre-modern period possessed a definite meaning for woman. The family and the Church both offered to women (in those days) fields of work which had been developed with some reference (however inadequate) to woman's own nature. She was at any rate credited with a character of her own.

It is the fact that, here and there, we see beginnings of a more positive conception of woman's life and functions. But characteristic of the whole crisis is the failure of these to develop into a definite nucleus for a new synthesis. Accordingly the general current of the Movement flows steadily towards "enfranchisement for freedom".

By a curious paradox, leaders of the Movement who were themselves orthodox in their moral outlook were amongst the foremost to raise the cry of freedom, and it was this cult which influenced their followers rather than their private religious and moral outlook. These same followers now use the idea of freedom as their chief weapon of attack upon marriage and the home. If their influence is increasing, it is not surprising. For their philosophy has the merit of consistency, whereas the leaders of the right wing have never freed themselves from the paralysing contradiction which is inherent in the attempt to combine the gospel of self-determination with the institution of monogamy (cf. p. 125).

From this standpoint we understand at once the comparative failure of the Woman's Movement—despite so much noble endeavour—really to achieve anything in the way of moral reform in the Christian sense. The Movement in its present form is part of a world-wide "process of dissolution", having its roots in the historical necessity of a rebellion against obsolete tyrannies; whereas Christianity, in its attitude towards sex problems, rests upon a wholly different basis from that of the philosophy of self-determination and ego-centricity.

.   .   .   .   .

Thus the general trend of the Movement, in spite of the unquestionable sincerity of its claim to be an agent of moral betterment, is (by virtue of a historical logic) such as to encourage a type of education and occupation, and a mental attitude towards life and towards the opposite sex, which works steadily against marriage and against the home.

This is no mere theorising. Where feminism has made progress the family has declined. Nowhere has the Woman's Movement been so active (or so intensely Puritan) as in the United States, a land in which divorce and the general break-up of monogamy has advanced with the most startling rapidity. If Judge Lindsey is a reliable witness, the young generation in America will go far beyond the present generation in its repudiation of monogamy. The conditions of what (from the Christian standpoint) can only be described as extreme sexual laxity, which he describes, have arisen in those very States which have long been under strong feminist influence. In Europe the lands least affected by feminism—such as Italy and Switzerland—are almost the sole surviving strongholds of the traditional Christian family life. Those who wish to study the peculiar conditions obtaining in Scandinavia, the historic home of feminism in Europe, should read *Feminism*, by Professor Wieth-Knudsen, in which the progressive disintegration of the home is described in full detail.

With respect to the moral situation an immense amount of sentimental, optimistic twaddle is uttered. Prominent men and women who ought to know much better are continually assuring the public that the emancipation of young people has inaugurated an era of cleaner morals, that the hypocrisy of the Victorian age has given way to a frank and "wholesome" attitude which promises a great moral improvement in the near future, and so on and so forth. As an antidote to this ostrich-like mentality—which is based upon pure ignorance of facts—readers of this book are counselled to make a study of the utterances of Judge B. Lindsey[1] (*The Revolt of Youth*), or of Professor Eberhard

---

[1] As an example of the sort of case which came before Judge Lindsey in his court for juveniles in Denver, at the rate of some 400 per annum, I may give the following: "Then there was the case of Ellen. Ellen, who is the daughter of a wealthy man in Denver, entered into an agreement with five other girls in the boarding-school she attended that she and they would each contrive to have a sex experience sometime during the summer vacation, so that they might compare notes in the fall. Ellen selected a boy, who had no thought of anything of the

(*Feminismus*: Vienna), in which works the real facts as to modern morality are revealed by those who know. Here we see clearly how swiftly the habit of forming temporary sex connections has spread amongst the populations of the "Western" lands during the last fifteen to twenty years. Conditions which, twenty years ago, would have shocked even those who were not particularly strait-laced, are now so common that they have practically ceased to attract attention.

sort, to take her to dinner in a restaurant, where they obtained a private room. There she seduced him, to his own utter astonishment. The boy was bewildered and amazed at what took place." Later, the question arose of whether or not her family should arrange for an abortion (of which about a thousand are supposed to take place yearly in Denver), but the Judge managed to get the baby placed discreetly, and later Ellen made a good marriage. The advocates of the companionate marriage idea propose to meet these "difficulties of youth" (a somewhat euphemistic term) by spreading far and wide a knowledge of contraceptive methods and making it legal for young couples to live together on trial for, say, two years, with option of renewal at the end of the period. (There is, of course, nothing magical about the number two; why not for one year or one month? Or why should not young girls go away for week-ends, taking their contraceptive outfit with them, and "trying-out" each of their boy friends, one after the other, until they found the right one? In this way they would surely cover the ground more quickly!) At any rate, this sort of thing is seriously put forward as sexual reform.

At an age when self-control and respect for womanhood are of basic importance for the development of mind and character, half-fledged youths and amorous schoolgirls are to be taught to play with contraceptives! Yet perhaps, after all, this is no more than the logical result of the cult of reckless independence. Another girl, asked by the Judge why she would not marry a boy with whom she had had sex relations, replied that she would not dream of tying herself to a boy who was not earning as much as she was herself.

I do not suggest that conditions are the same in Great Britain as in Denver; but we are dealing with a world-wide phenomenon. On the Continent, in extensive social circles, amazing sexual laxity prevails, and if these customs are as yet not so widespread in England, that is due largely to our insular position, which causes world-tendencies to arrive later.

It is quite idle to approach the problems of this chapter in a state of illusion as to the actual situation. Sooner or later the friends and supporters of the Woman's Movement will have to make up their minds whether they think it worth while to follow the path outlined in this chapter and make a serious attempt to build up the family, or whether they will let things slide.

.   .   .   .   .

Let there be no possibility of misunderstanding. It is true that the Movement contains a great multitude of earnest religious women, who err rather through an excess of Puritanism than through any tendency to laxity. But are they in control of the situation, or are they borne along on the surface? A restless urge towards liberty, in the vaguest possible sense of the term, is the life-breath of the Movement.[1]

Take the much-discussed question of the "single-standard" in morals. This has always been interpreted by the religious section of the Movement as meaning that men should be raised to the same moral level as that previously imposed upon women. Most supporters of women's emancipation still regard it in this light. But what do we find? In the circles most affected by feminist doctrines the equalisation of the moral standard is being attempted *in the reverse sense*— women are making haste to claim for themselves the same freedom to indulge in sex relationships outside marriage formerly granted (at any rate in some degree) to men.

[1] At the very moment of writing this section I see in the leading daily organ of British Nonconformity an article by a woman in which she says: "What is this emancipation of which we talk so glibly? The word means simply freedom from moral and intellectual fetters!" ("Are Women Free?" by Nina Condron, in the *Daily News* of October 19, 1928.) There is no explanation of what is meant by "freedom from moral fetters"—it might mean anything or nothing!

Moreover, as Oskar Schmitz most pertinently remarks, there is a big difference. The sexual laxity more usually associated with the male sex was never, in Christian lands, accepted as an ideal, although it may have been tolerated under protest. But the sexual liberty claimed by our advanced feminists is put forward as an ideal. It is held to be a solemn *right* to which the emancipated woman is entitled. This is an infinitely more serious menace to monogamy than the sort of half-hearted tolerance of male promiscuity which existed, and still exists, in man-made society; also for the further reason that the attitude of women towards moral problems is more important than the attitude of men, since women are the special custodians of the family and the tone-setting influence in society. Further, when men ruled, women did not admit a male right to sexual freedom, but the new feminists demand from men full acquiescence in the freedom of the female.[1] (A special feature of the crisis is the remarkable absence of strong protest against such views, even in England. Recent feminist publications in this sense have been favourably received by the Press, even by leading organs of sober middle-class opinion and by religious papers.)

When confronted with such arguments as the foregoing, many feminists reply: "Yes, we know the family is going. Let it go. We are going to build up a new and better morality upon its ruins." This may sound very fine, but in sober truth is there even the slightest guarantee that free-love, or polygamy, or promiscuity, or whatever we shall

---

[1] This tendency is not denied by leading feminists. In *Time and Tide* (October 19, 1928) Miss Cicely Hamilton, after explaining that the emancipation of women will make them less intuitive, goes on to say: "In a world that, of late, has greatly changed, it is unlikely that intuition will be the only womanly characteristic to register a decline; there are signs that, in the matter of sexual morality, the code of women—of ordinary women—is likely to be amended in the direction of laxity."

get in place of the family, will give us a sound basis for our social life?

We cannot here digress to take up the question of monogamy *versus* the "new morality", but it is essential that we should try to see where we are going. From the point of view of those who seek to destroy the family, the present situation does not present any cause for alarm. On the other hand, if we desire to save the family we must rouse ourselves to the necessity of reviewing critically the whole drift of modern feminine education, occupation, and emancipation.

A merely negative attitude would, however, be worse than useless. The Woman's Movement is a great historical fact. It cannot be denied and it cannot be frustrated. It is folly to dream of putting the clock back.

If monogamy is to be saved, it cannot be by a return to outworn forms, but only in the sense envisaged by Keyserling (in his noteworthy book on Marriage), by a re-orientation which, without abandoning the monogamous principle, gives it new vitality by relating it to our ideal of an enlarged and self- and race-conscious womanhood.

The reaction against marriage is due largely to the inadequacy of the opportunities which it offers to the modern girl. In recent newspaper controversies upon the modern girl and her attitude towards life, the view was expressed again and again that the well-paid woman worker of to-day does not desire to marry because she is so often better off where she is. Why should a girl earning four pounds a week, and enjoying a comfortable free life, give all this up in order to marry a man who is barely earning as much as she is herself?

Modern conditions, and not the least the influence of feminism, have thus brought about a reversal of the natural order of things. In place of the line of natural function seeming desirable, the line of abstention from function has

P

been made to seem (at any rate) the more desirable. Starting with the idea that the hard lot of the unmarried woman must be alleviated, the process has now gone so far that her lot has been made more attractive than that of the married woman, and especially than that of the mother of a family. But unless we actually desire the decline of the race, such a position is fatal.

A revision of our social ideals, *in a racial sense*, followed up by far-reaching social reconstruction, can alone be effective at the present stage.

As stated at the very beginning of this work, the central fact of the present situation is that the emancipation of women has created new problems of portentous significance for our civilisation. No one would now say that the mere fact of this emancipation gives us a higher type of society. All depends upon *the use which is made of the new liberties*.

That woman simply as woman, by virtue of her sex alone, will bring some healing influence into the modern chaos is an optimistic illusion. Many of the most sophistical and demoralising utterances in modern literature come from female pens. And in great centres of civilisation, where women wield a far greater power than they have ever before possessed, we witness a degree of licence in manners and morals such as Western life has not seen for generations.[1]

[1] The *Reichspost* of Vienna (January 6, 1928) recently published an able review of the present standing of the Woman's Movement in Central Europe, in the course of which it referred to the "grotesque contrast" between the newly attained dignity of woman in public affairs and the accompanying collapse of womanly dignity in the field of manners and conduct, and in contemporary art and literature. In the same age that has given us women members of Parliament and women in positions of influence in every field of life, in literature and upon the stage, we see such a glorification of immorality and perversity as we have never before experienced. The Movement has "completely failed to improve the moral situation"—a state of things attributed largely to the decline of home-life and to the refusal of women leaders to recognise economical, physical, and psychological realities.

The supreme need of the age is wise leadership. But it is not easy to see how those can lead who have no clear aims. Therefore, at the present stage, nothing matters more than a calm and objective consideration of the position, a process of intellectual and moral stocktaking. Where do we stand? Where do we intend to go?

Do we propose to drift along in a current we cannot control towards an end we do not know, or do we propose to face the situation purposefully? In the latter case we must work out a new social synthesis, on the one hand assigning to women a larger and more inspiring field of work, and on the other delimiting, much more precisely than is now the case, the boundaries of woman's (and man's) rights and moral liberties.

e. THE RACE QUESTION

From the foregoing we pass, by a natural transition, to a brief consideration of the race question proper.

The most outstanding development in present-day Western civilisation is the gradual decline, in a racial sense, of the superior stocks.

It is true that an endless controversy rages as to the precise meaning of the word "superior". The orthodox democrat becomes infuriated at the mere suggestion that all sections of the population are not equal in their character and ability, and does not hesitate to accuse the eugenists of being inhuman stud-farmers. But however difficult it may be to assign a satisfactory definition to the term "superior", we cannot, in the light of modern research into the history of stocks and into the mental make-up of various strata of society, refuse the idea that there are sections oɪ the nation in which a high level of ability is much more frequently to be found than in others. We also know definitely that the latter sections are immensely more prolific than the former (by this is meant not merely that their birth-rate is higher, but that the number of surviving children is larger, after allowing for a higher death-rate in these classes).

In writing the foregoing I do not, of necessity, commit myself to the position of the out-and-out eugenists. The whole question is full of difficulties. It might be almost impossible under present conditions to contemplate any such thing as deliberate breeding from better stocks. It might, too, be most dangerous to attempt any interference with the domestic life of the supposedly inferior elements.

But one thing is certain. It is undesirable that any existing human material, *known to be first class*, should be allowed to pass into extinction. We possess in Great Britain to-day magnificent stocks, of proved quality and intelligence. We know, further, that these stocks are in a state of racial decline (i.e. their annual output of children does not suffice to balance their annual death-roll).

Our professional optimists soothe us with the argument that there is an inexhaustible reservoir of ability in the lowest classes, and that we need not worry in the least about the dwindling numbers of the so-called superior stocks. But even if we admit that much latent ability is hidden away in the lowest classes, the question arises: How long can we draw upon this reserve before it will be exhausted? Stocks rising through superior ability and passing into the higher social levels soon acquire the habits of infertility which are there prevalent, and in their turn pass into extinction. As Professor F. C. S. Schiller writes:

"The ultimate reward of merit [i.e. in our type of society] is sterilisation, and society appears to be an organisation devoted to the suicidal task of extirpating any ability it may chance to contain, by draining it away from any stratum in which it may occur, promoting it to the highest, and there destroying it. It is exactly as though a dairyman should set in motion apparatus for separating the cream from the milk, and then as it rose skim it off and throw it away!" (*Tantalus: or the Future of Man*, Section VI.)

It must be transparently obvious that, even upon the above assumption (of the existence of large reserves of ability), we shall in the future be far worse off with dwindling stocks amongst the present educated classes than if we were to possess both the able members of these stocks *and* the able who may rise from the "inexhaustible reservoir".

In regarding the matter thus, we are taking the most optimistic view possible. In reality it has not been proved that there is any such immense reserve of undiscovered ability amongst our agricultural labourers and slum-dwellers. That occasional individuals arise from these strata and make their way forward is admitted by everyone; but we have no substantial proof that there exist in these lowest (and alone adequately fertile) classes reserves capable of replacing the large diminution now taking place in the ranks of the cultured classes. And if such reserves do not exist, we are faced with the certainty that the general level of ability will, in the future, sink with considerable rapidity.[1]

[1] It would be possible to produce a mass of statistics to support the above statements, but it is hardly necessary. It is now known that the vast majority of families in the more educated classes (and even in the superior artisan class) are declining in numbers. W. C. D. Whetham, Carr-Saunders, Dr. Sutherland, and others have produced overwhelming evidence to this effect. In *Race Hygiene and Heredity*, by Dr. H. W. Siemens (published by Appleton), some of the most recent figures are to be found. Dr. Siemens analyses the history of his own family. Over a number of generations the number of children per marriage was as follows: 5, 5, 5·8, 5, 5·3, 6, 4·8, 3·7, 2·8—the fertility of the family being now insufficient to keep its numbers constant. In England the decline has been from round about six children per family two generations ago to two and even less than two to-day (in the cultured classes).

There are, indeed, already not a few signs of a marked dearth of outstanding mental ability. The whole subject is now in the stage of investigation. But the great body of scientific opinion most certainly supports the contention that the natural hereditary ability of the educated classes is superior to that of the lowest classes—it is not merely that the children of the former obtain better environment, better food, and so forth, and thus, by virtue of these advantages, attain a higher mental level (as alleged by the opponents of the eugenic position).[1] The tendency to over-value education, and to be blind to the immense inborn differences of capacity in different individuals and strains, is all part of the rationalistic unpsychological life-outlook which is now becoming obsolete. Indeed, when we consider that a process of social sifting, by which the more able stocks

In the lowest classes the families are more than twice as large. In the poorest parts of the London East End the birth-rates are upwards of 30 per 1,000, and in the West End round about 10 per 1,000. Or taking Glasgow, we find that in Mile End (a poor part) the birth-rate is 31, and in Cathcart (a good residential district) it is 10·2 (it is important to note that the death-rates are respectively 17·5 and 8·7, so that the difference between birth-rate and death-rate, determining the increase, is 13·5 in the one case and only 1·5 in the other; the increase in the poorest class in Glasgow is thus seen to be nine times more rapid than in the better middle class. (Strictly speaking, this is an underestimate, since Cathcart also contains lower-class elements, and if these were to be allowed for, we should find an actual decrease.) It must not be forgotten that these effects are cumulative, and increase immensely in successive generations. A stock with a birth-rate of, say, 15 per 1,000 will be swamped in four generations by a stock with a rate of 25 per 1,000. It is thus clear that the future ability and character of the nation will be determined not only largely, *but almost completely*, by the hereditary qualities of those who now constitute the very lowest section of the population.

[1] The reader is referred to the publications of the Eugenics Society, and the works of Karl Pearson, Galton, Woods, Schuster, Peters, L. Darwin, H. W. Siemens, Carr-Saunders, amongst others. An important German work is Baur-Fischer-Lenz' *Grundriss der menschlichen Erblichkeitslehre*.

have gravitated upwards in the social scale, has been going on in England for centuries, it is natural enough that the upper strata of society should show superior ability (by upper strata is meant not the moneyed or titled classes, but, in a much wider sense, all those occupying positions for which definite ability is needed—the village schoolmaster is in an upper class, as compared with the day-labourer).

.   .   .   .   .

Even if we do not consider an increase of population desirable for the nation as a whole, this is no valid reason for regarding the extinction of the best stocks with equanimity. On the contrary, the smaller the nation the more important that its quality should be maintained. Yet the argument that we do not require any increase of population is very frequently brought forward (especially by feminists) in order to justify their non-racial ideals of marriage and the family. It is stated that the modern highly educated woman need not have children, as we are already overpopulated, the inference being that this is a matter which can safely be left to the lower classes, while the girl of the most intelligent stocks goes in for aviation, engineering, or politics. At any rate, whether this be meant or not, this is what is taking place.

We see here, as in so many other aspects of the problem Woman and Society, that there is a great gulf between theory and practice. The theory of the birth-control optimists is that birth-control should be taught to the whole nation, and that it will then be employed in a eugenic sense; the healthy people of the best stocks will have large families, and those who are tainted, or whose heredity is inferior, will limit their offspring, the quality of the race being thus improved. But in practice there is not the faintest indication that the situation is developing along these lines. Quite the reverse. Birth-control is being taken up with enthusiasm by the best stocks, who are declining; while the fertility of the inferior stocks remains much higher (even although they, too, often restrict their families to a lesser extent). The mere fact that marriage takes place earlier amongst the wage-earning class, combined with the provision of facilities for education, medical treatment, and so forth, will suffice to maintain the rate in this class at a higher level, even were birth-control to be universal.

We thus arrive at the conclusion that the building up of family life amongst the best sections of the population is by far the most vital matter. *And it is precisely in this direction that little or nothing is being done.*

Although shortage of space compels me to pass over the population question proper (the question as to the possible or desirable population of these islands, or of the world), it is essential to touch upon these points in this section, if only to refute the objection (which I anticipate in the minds of some readers) that in our supposedly overpopulated land it is quite unnecessary to make any attempt to build up the family. The preservation of our best English strains is of vital import, apart altogether from the wider matter of the desirability or otherwise of a general increase of population.

Supposing we admit that for the Western races a further considerable increase of population does not appear desirable—and this would seem to be the conclusion which such peoples as the French and the Anglo-Saxons have arrived at for themselves—it does not, however, follow that other races (possibly looked upon by us as lower) will think along the same lines. They may believe, and some of them do believe, that their development is only just beginning. Such races will refuse the idea of limiting their population, and will increase in the future by leaps and bounds. As examples we may take Japan and Italy. Mussolini, as we know, is straining every nerve to encourage the Italian people to expand. With the Japanese, the idea of the race is a religion, and they have every intention of expanding to three or four times their present population. Even in Germany, although the Germans are more under the influence of Western ideas on the subject of population than either of the other two peoples, there is a very large section of the nation which entirely rejects the idea of a drastic limitation of population, and conceives of the race as destined to an immense future expansion. In Russia there is a prodigious increase of population, amounting to more than two million per annum. In fifty years, if this continues, the Russians will total some 250 millions, as against, say, 39 million French and 40 million English (supposing the latter races to follow their present policy of limitation). At the end of the same period the Japanese would number some 110 millions, and the Germans possibly about 100 millions. It would be impossible to deny that such a prospect presents catastrophic possibilities. It may be said that there is no room for such an expansion. But it was said a hundred years ago that the population of England could never pass beyond the 30 million mark. The world contains land enough for such a development—Siberia is almost untouched, South America contains vast potentialities, the British Dominions are only very partially developed, and in the absence of British stock will fill up rapidly with aliens. Here again, in short, we see a wide gulf between the optimistic theories of many social reformers and actual possibilities. It may be believed (or perhaps rather *hoped*) that peoples like the Japanese will embrace our views as to population. But is there the slightest guarantee that they will do anything of the kind? And what will be the political

and economic situation of the Western races, even in so
short a period as fifty years, if they do not?

.   .   .   .   .

Are the leaders and inspirers of the Woman's Movement
of to-day fully alive to the realities of the situation?

It is true that here and there one finds a recognition of
the all-important rôle which woman must play if we are
to solve the tremendous problem raised by our dysgenic
breeding. (I leave on one side the other issue, of national
population, which cannot here be adequately examined.)
But we miss any suggestion of a definite constructive
approach to the problem.[1]

Professor McDougall deals impressively in his *Social
Psychology* with the antithesis between individual liberty
and social sanctions, and shows us how crucial a part this
question has played in the crises of past civilisations. Does
the Woman's Movement offer us an effective solution to
this problem, or does it merely preach individual emancipation and leave society to look after itself? Much will depend
on the answer to this question.

A complete re-orientation of the Movement, bringing
it into close touch with racial issues, will be needful if it is
to clear itself from such charges as those brought by S. H.
Halford (quoted by McDougall in *National Welfare and
National Decay*), that if the ideals of feminism were to be
realised the best intelligence of Britain and America would

[1] The standard works of the Woman's Movement are full of in-
accurate and thoroughly misleading statements upon all that relates
to the family and the race. Olive Schreiner actually thought that the
lower death-rate in the middle and upper classes compensated for the
lower birth-rate; and Mrs. C. P. Gilman entertained the amazing
idea that an average of two children per marriage would suffice to
maintain the population (the actual number is, of course, between
$3 \cdot 5$ and $4 \cdot 0$, according to the conditions). As a matter of fact, none of
the earlier feminists devoted the slightest attention to racial questions.

be extinct in three generations; and by Professor Max Wolf (the German authority on population questions), that the racial decay of the best German middle class is due, not only partially, but *mainly* to the spread of feminist ideas.

Further, if we consider those sections of modern society which have been most deeply affected by the emancipationist doctrines, it is at once obvious that they are in a state of decay, in a racial sense. In most of the large cities of the United States (especially where Roman Catholicism is not strong) the annual excess of deaths over births (even so far down in the social scale as the superior hand-working class) is very considerable. The same applies to Berlin, Hamburg, Vienna, or London. (On the other hand, in Rome, Milan, Madrid, and many other great centres but little affected by feminism, the fertility of all classes is adequate.) While it would not be fair to lay the sole blame for this state of things at the door of feminism, its influence, direct and indirect, is of great significance in reducing fertility.

The (more or less) feminist communities of to-day would appear to exist *in parasitic fashion*, by drawing continually upon the superior racial vitality of other sections of the community. Thus the population of Berlin could not be maintained at all by means of the children of the emancipated Berlin women, but must absorb fresh material from the country-side, where women have not yet learned the lessons of feminism.

f. FORWARD PATHS

Clear in the conviction that we have departed far from the norm of a healthy society, let us ask ourselves the question: What can we do to get back to a better way of life?

As Mr. Ludovici says, women have given up "living a life" in order to earn a living. The expansion of feminine careers has been accompanied by a continual diminution in woman's racial interests and opportunities, by a corresponding shrinkage in the breadth and importance of the personal side of life. Do we seriously propose to find a way out of this dilemma? And if so, by what paths?

It has already been seen that everything turns around the question of values. It is the triumph of a narrow masculinism, with all its indifference to the family and the race, that has brought us to the present impasse. And it is the failure of the modern woman to value highly enough woman's specific character and her racial tasks that has, more than anything else, enabled the technical-mechanical life-outlook to win such an astonishing triumph over the whole of the positive feminine side of life.

Our salvation consists in returning to the ancient truth that a division of labour between the sexes is intended in the scheme of evolution; that their faculties being *complementary*, they do not, in Dr. Arabella Kenealy's words, "normally come into rivalry and antagonism in the fulfilment of their respective life-rôles." It is, as Olive Schreiner urged, more especially the shrinkage in woman's sphere that has driven her to seek new (and for the most part much less fertile) pastures. And it is by a purposeful attempt to rebuild the feminine side of life, while at the same time keeping open the new careers which have been won for women, that we can best advance towards a social construction that is racially sound.

Our aim is simple and clear. It is the establishment of a state of society in which there should be the most useful and harmonious division of labour possible between the sexes— a state giving to women, as to men, the fullest and freest opportunities for self-development, each sex in accordance with its own inborn talents and aptitudes. If we assume it to be true, and no doubt it is true, that the average man attains his fullest development through some typical career, such as engineering, sailoring, or the practice of a learned profession, and the average woman through a suitable marriage, then it follows that the improvement of marriage opportunities for women will be one of the most vital factors in the bringing about of such a society. While not losing sight of this aim, we must not neglect the interests of those women who belong to the million or so who are numerically in excess, or who, for one reason or another, do not wish to marry, or have found no suitable mates. For the army of single women we must aim at creating openings of all sorts which shall give them occupation in accordance with their own tastes and specific gifts. As far as is humanly possible, given the difficult conditions of modern industrialism, they must be emancipated from underpaid, monotonous slavery in factories, workshops, and offices, and transferred to more fruitful and congenial fields oι labour. Above all, they must receive remuneration which will place their work on a higher level and give it a greater weight in the balance of our common life.

.   .   .   .   .

It is, in the first place, needful to break away from the present vicious circle of low wages, cheap female labour, employment of large numbers of married women, unemployed men, high taxes to support the unemployed men, the depression of trade by high taxes, the lowering of wages still further through trade depression, and so on and so on, each link in the chain pulling at the next link, and all dragging the nation downwards.

Under present conditions (assuming a Government with powers no greater than those now wielded) it would no doubt be the best policy to attack several of these points simultaneously, since they are all closely linked up.

A vigorous housing policy, combined with the introduction of the Family Wage System in one form or another, would do much to promote the marriage-rate. It is needful to point out, however, that this system, if it is not to function dysgenically, must not be confined to the wage-earning classes. Members of the salaried class, wherever it is in the least possible, should be paid on the same principle. Otherwise there is a danger that the Family Wage would merely encourage the birth-rate amongst the working-class, where such an encouragement is much less necessary instead of assisting the young brain-worker to found a family. We must avoid taking any steps which would tend still further to increase the discrepancy (already far too great) in birth-rates between the hand-workers and the brain-workers.

With respect to the housing question, we should avoid taking the narrow view that every housing scheme should be an immediate financial success. It might pay well, in the long run, to build, say, half a million or more houses, and let them at rents which would not yield more than 2 or 3 per cent. on the capital. If the building were done through the large municipalities, the Government could provide a system of loans to cover the actual losses. The benefit to the nation, through improved trade, the betterment of family life, and through the hygienic advantage to the people, would far outweigh the loss, which could not amount to more than the cost of a cruiser or two yearly.

In connection with the question of raising wages, it is obvious that it will be of the greatest importance to introduce up-to-date machinery in all branches of industry and to improve methods of production and work in every way. It is thus possible that many factories now employing cheap female labour could be so reorganised, and without any diminution of profits, as to employ men paid a good wage. Much can be learned from American methods in this field of experience. We must do our best to get beyond the state of things in which inefficiently managed concerns keep up their position by employing underpaid girls. This is one of the worst evils in the chain which we are attempting to break through.

With regard to the third point, sociologists have again and again drawn attention to the evils resulting from the employment of married women. Here it should be possible to insist more strictly than has up to now been the case upon the observance of the various suggestions which have constantly been put forward by hygienic authorities, with the object of insisting upon proper periods of rest for married women before and after childbirth. In view of the evidence brought forward by medical men (see, for example, Havelock Ellis's work, *Sex in Relation to Society*), it is certain that the rest period should not be less than at least three months prior to the birth. If these hygienic considerations were to be given full weight, we should probably, as a result, see a considerable diminution in the number of married women workers. Moreover, in the case of all groups of employment in which it can be definitely shown that the work unfavourably influences the health of the children, there should be no hesitation in forbidding altogether the employment of married women. *The racial point of view must make itself felt more and more*, even at the risk of causing some dislocation of existing methods of work and organisation. It would be well if all our educational authorities became more aware of the supreme importance of securing the health of children even before they are born. It would in many cases be then much less necessary to resort to the feeding and medical treatment which are now instituted by many educational bodies. In those cases where actual poverty compels women to leave the home and go into the factory or the tailor's shop, it should be possible to raise the husband's wages up to the subsistence level (if needful through governmental control), and, in the long run, this would be far less expensive than the employment of the wives under unsuitable conditions. It goes without saying that none of these problems can be hopefully tackled until we have fully shaken off the influence of Victorian individualism in the industrial field, with its wholly non-racial outlook. The married woman worker is something more than a unit in the system of industry: she is *the vehicle of the race*, and as such must be guarded against both the economic tendency to exploit her inferior standing and the scarcely less dangerous equalitarian feminist tendency to look upon her just as if she were a male worker.

·   ·   ·   ·   ·

Further, we should be concerned with the development of fields of work specially congenial to women and offering them opportunities of self-realisation superior to those obtainable, in general, under existing conditions. *Here, in particular, positive feminism can do a great work.*

The gradual decline in the sale and popularity of the mass-made Ford car in America and elsewhere was the sign of a very wholesome desire on the part of the public to possess cars with more individuality and of a superior artistic style. But why should this welcome movement stop at motor cars? Why should not the buying public revolt against factory-made furniture, pottery, or metal fittings? A well-known British architect recently expressed the view that men will spend large sums of money on buying tasteful and individual cars, but grudge every pound spent in designing and fitting up houses to suit their fancy, being

in this department of life quite content to accept the mass-
made and soulless article of the cheap building contractor.
This is a profoundly true remark. An immense field of
work lies open to those who could organise the training
and employment of really artistic workers in the production
of personally designed furniture, metal-work (e.g. lamps,
gas-brackets, taps, bells, knockers, signs, switches), wood-
work, domestic fittings of all sorts, leather-work, pottery,
fabrics, clothing, garden requisites, motor-car fittings, and
so forth. If the public can be educated up to paying for cars
a much higher price than that needful for the utility article,
we need not despair of raising it to the point of buying
tasteful and interesting furniture or metal-work. There are
already promising signs, especially in Germany, Austria,
and Scandinavia, of an awakening in this respect. There is
no reason at all why artistic work in objects of utility should
be looked upon as a fad. We may hope for an age when every
man will aim at possessing objects of real beauty round about
him, as was indeed the case before the industrial age set in.
In Austria, Italy, and elsewhere, there are still thousands
of old houses where every fitting, down to the taps of the
water-pipes, is a separate work of art. It might not be practicable at the present moment to employ more than a
limited number of persons at this kind of work, but a movement of this kind, once started and accompanied by a
vigorous campaign of advertisement and public education,
might take us a long way.

It is scarcely necessary to say that this kind of work is
quite peculiarly suitable for girls and women. It need not
be carried out under conditions so arduous and uninteresting
as those of the usual factory. To take a single example: in
a small country place near London an artist opened, some
twenty years ago, a small workshop for hand-made metal
goods, and in time was able to employ some twenty women

workers, under almost perfect conditions as regards health. A development of this kind of work would be most valuable in creating opportunities for women workers. Theoretically there would be room for the employment of hundreds of thousands of workers, but, in practice, progress must, of course, depend upon the expansion of the market.

The advantages attaching to developments along these lines are manifold. We should create healthy employment, where it did not compete unduly with masculine lines of work, give to a large number of girls and women work offering them far better opportunities of personal interest and harmonious self-development than those obtainable in factories or business houses, and last, but not least, we should be taking a long step towards freeing ourselves from the tyranny of the mass-made impersonal article of modern commerce. One might almost say that there is a superfluity of able and energetic women in modern England. If a number of these were to employ their energy in expanding this fruitful field of work, they would be performing a national service of incalculable value.

In another chapter I refer to the error underlying the assumption in *Woman and Labour* and kindred feminist works that we have now entered upon a mechanical era, and that woman has no alternative but to adapt herself to the machine. As a matter of fact, the hey-day of the utilitarian age is over. There are now numerous signs of an awakening to the need for saving as much as possible of the human and personal side of life from the wheels of the machine. This does not mean that we can or should go back to an age of hand-work and dispense with machinery. That is Utopian nonsense. It is, however, possible to use machinery without being enslaved by it. No one with any common sense would suggest that we should abandon railways, motor cars, or electricity. Nor would it be practicable to give up mass production in factories for many articles of daily use, which it would be much too laborious to produce by hand—such as knives and forks, bottles, the cheaper kinds of clothing and boots, and so on. But there is room within the present era of technical science for an immense expansion of artistic hand-work, provided that public opinion supports it. It ought, indeed, to be part of the function of sex-conscious women (that is, women who realise that a will-less absorption in the dreary technicalities of modern industry is not consonant with their highest ideal of womanhood) systematically to educate public taste in this direction; and this they can well do through their boundless influence in all matters relating to the home and its appurtenances.

. . . . .

We are to-day realising, more and more, that we have much to learn from the Guild System of the pre-Reformation period. Progress takes place rather in spirals, ascending to higher levels, than in straight lines, and progress to-day consists more in returning, on a new level (with all the advantages of machinery and science), to the organic social ideals of the mediæval period, than in going blindly forward in a direct continuation of the present reckless individualism.

In the thirteenth and fourteenth centuries, in spite of the large excess of women, the sex problem was less acute than it is to-day; and this was partially due to the careful organisation of society in Guilds. In Germany, at that time, there were some sixty-five types of occupation reserved entirely for women, and some eighty for men, as well as about sixty open to both sexes.[1] We might do much worse than take a hint from this wise arrangement. Certain lines of work—the nature of which has been to some extent indicated in the foregoing—might be specially developed in the interests

[1] K. Bücher, *Die Frauenfrage im Mittelalter.*

of women workers, who would receive preferential treatment. This would be only fair to women, in view of the superior opportunities of men in such walks of life as engineering, the law, sailoring, and so forth. If these occupations were to be closely organised and connected with a system of training-colleges and technical schools, it might be practicable to raise immensely the standard of our work in these occupations.

There is in reality no lack of professions and occupations psychologically suitable for young women. No one imagines that it is possible to make a clear distinction; there must, of course, be much overlapping; but it would greatly assist the task of educational orientation and social organisation if we did our best to delimit spheres of influence, and, as far as is reasonably possible, send the yearly stream of young women leaving school and college into these fields of work, rather than pour it indiscriminately into the labour market, without the slightest regard either to economic possibilities or to human factors.

In the first place we have the traditional spheres :

Nursing (hospital, private, children's nurses, etc.) : according to the *Memorandum on Openings and Trainings for Women* (published by the London and National Society for Women's Service), the demand for properly trained children's nurses far exceeds the supply, and the importance to the community of this grossly underrated branch of work cannot be over-emphasised.

Infant Teaching, Kindergarten Work, Crèche Work, etc.: a great deal remains to be done in the development of these lines of work.

Domestic Service (including cooking, housekeeping, and so forth) in private homes and in institutions: here, too, the demand exceeds the supply; and if this line of work, so indispensable to the whole life of the nation, were raised to a higher level, it would be capable of absorbing a large number of women and girls.

Catering (restaurant, hotel, boarding-house, and tea-room work): there is here a very considerable area of employ-ment, and one by no means fully developed.

Dressmaking, Millinery, Sewing, etc.: the great majority of workers in this very large field will always be women, and there does not appear to be any very good reason why men should ever have been allowed to gain a footing; a more scientific training of women in this line should enable them to regain some of the higher branches now partly in the hands of men. In this department we may include shops for women's goods, where more women and fewer men might well be em-ployed.

In the second place we have several more recent fields of work for women, as yet by no means fully developed:

Medical Work (including midwifery, dental work, dentistry, and health visitors, etc.): undoubtedly there is here a very extensive field for women, and one only partially developed. There are some branches of the medical profession peculiarly suited for women, who might well specialise in the diseases of women and children; and it has recently been pointed out how much we require a more scientific development of midwifery. New training-colleges for women (possibly aided by public funds) are needed in this field. Clinics of various kinds are urgently needed in many of our large centres, and a considerable number of women workers might be employed in connection with these.

Teaching will, of course, continue to furnish wide openings
for women, but is perhaps less capable of further extension than many other fields here mentioned, since there
is already a somewhat excessive proportion of women
teachers, especially in the elementary schools. It is not
at all desirable that the teaching profession should
become (as in the United States) almost a female
monopoly.

Government Inspectors (of factories, workshops, sanitary conditions, etc.) : there is a very considerable field for the employment of women as inspectors; many of the existing
women inspectors are said to be seriously overworked.

Social Welfare Work : this is an elastic term, covering several
departments in which there is scope for women; for
example, work amongst children, club and settlement
work, work as relieving officers, in the organisation of
juvenile employment, in play-centres, in crèches,
amongst the blind, crippled, deaf and dumb and mentally defective. In this wide field there is room for a
great expansion of women's activities, given an effective
organisation.

Religious Work : although some of the Churches have opened
their doors to women ministers, it is hardly likely that
any very large increase in the number of women
preachers will take place. But there is an extensive field
for important work to be done by women in close relation with ministers of religion, in schools, as rescue
workers, deaconesses, mission workers, and so on. In the
Catholic Church the rôle of the sisters is most essential,
and in Protestant circles much remains to be done to
fill up a gap in this direction, thereby balancing the
one-sided masculinism to which reference was made in
section *b*.

Architecture (with house-decoration and furnishing): it is
fairly obvious that this is a field of work offering particularly good opportunities for women to turn to good
use their natural interest in the home and its beautifica-
tion, and much can be done to open up new careers for
women in this direction. The rather surprising fact that
women did not earlier take advantage of the numerous
opportunities here offered is to be explained chiefly
through the over-intellectualism of the Feminist Movement.

Literature, Music, Dramatic Art, Painting, Sculpture, Dancing, fall
into a somewhat different category from any of the
above activities, since the gifts needful for success are
here so wholly individual; and it is upon their gifts alone
that the progress of women in the specifically artistic
lines of work must depend. It goes without saying that
there must be equality of opportunity. The great significance of arts and crafts for women's work has been
specially emphasised above.

Agriculture reveals very considerable opportunities for women,
more especially in its lighter branches, e.g. fruit-growing,
market-gardening, dairy-farming, poultry-keeping, bee-
keeping, stock-breeding, and every sort of gardening.
In view of the comparative shortage of labour upon the
land and the general lack of intensive culture in
England, this department is well worth developing. It
would seem possible for a great many more girls and
women to find work in this field.

Secretarial and Library Work afford opportunities which are of
importance, although these departments are somewhat
overcrowded at present.

The above is an incomplete list of the various occupations

which are specially "indicated", as the doctors would say, for girls and women. There are, of course, many other lines of work which are open to women. With regard to certain other categories, we might say that they are contra-indicated; for example, sailoring, machine-work, engineering, mining, puddling and blast-furnace work, railway service, bus and tram driving, as well as certain professions, such as accountancy, banking, insurance, law, and the Civil Service, where the presence of women does not appear particularly valuable, although there should be nothing done to prevent individual women trying their luck along these lines if they wish. They are not, however, to be recommended for the average girl.

With regard to the immense field of work open to women in factories and offices, it will be clear from the foregoing that much would be gained if female labour was here employed as little as possible. Most of this work is soul-destroying and unhygienic, and it has no special contacts with feminine needs or aptitudes.

.   .   .   .   .

It would take us too far afield to examine in detail the various possibilities of woman's work in the world of to-day; but it will be abundantly clear from the foregoing that, granting a definite feminine psychology no less important than the masculine, the core of the whole matter lies in preserving and strengthening this psychology, and enabling women, in the first place, to realise themselves; and, in the second place, to bring their ripest gifts to bear upon the world. We must never lose sight of the idea of bi-polarity. I know of no truer words in this connection than those which stand at the head of this chapter, spoken by one of the finest minds of our age.

The problem is certainly not easy. It cannot be solved

merely by letting things slide. *We must make a real attempt to think the matter out and get back to first principles.* If women have a definite contribution to make to human culture, let it be our conscious aim to modify education and occupation in the light of this idea.

This section will have served its purpose if it has indicated a wrong path and a right path. The wrong path is to encourage the absorption of women in the soulless machinery of a technical and industrial age. The right way is to aim steadfastly at the expansion and elevation (moral and financial) of all those fields of life and work which can provide opportunities of self-realisation for women.

BIBLIOGRAPHY

IT would, of course, be impossible to provide anything like a full bibliography of such a wide subject as Woman and Society. In its absence, it is hoped that the following suggestions for further reading will be of value to students.

Numerous further references will be found in many of the works mentioned below—especially in those by Wieth-Knudsen, Heymans, and Tandler and Gross.

The Subjection of Women, John Stuart Mill.

Woman and Labour, Olive Schreiner.

Women and Economics, Mrs. C. P. Gilman.

The Cause, Mrs. R. Strachey.

A Short History of Women, Langdon Davies.

The Vocation of Woman, Mrs. Archibald Colquhoun.

Hypatia: or Woman and Knowledge, Mrs. Bertrand Russell.

The Woman's Movement, Ellen Key.

A Survey of the Woman Problem, Rosa Mayreder.

Feminism and Sex Extinction, Dr. A. Kenealy.

Woman: a Vindication, A. M. Ludovici.

Man: an Indictment, A. M. Ludovici.

Woman Adrift, Harold Owen.

In Defence of Women, H. L. Mencken.

Feminism, Professor Wieth-Knudsen (with bibliography).

Feminismus und Kulturuntergang, E. F. W. Eberhard (Braumüller: Vienna).

Wespennester, O. A. H. Schmitz.

The Ethics of Feminism, A. R. Wadia.

. . . .

The Dominant Sex: a Study in the Sociology of Sex Differentiation, Mathilde and Mathias Vaerting.

Adolescence: its Psychology and its Relation to Physiology, Anthropology, Sex, Crime, Religion, and Education, G. Stanley Hall.

Studies in the Psychology of Sex, Havelock Ellis.

Die Psychologie der Frauen, Dr. G. Heymans (Winter: Heidelberg)— translation from the Dutch (with bibliography).

Die biologischen Grundlagen der sekundären Geschlechts-charaktere, Tandler und Gross (with large bibliography).

Psychische Geschlechtsunterschiede, Otto Lipmann (Barth: Leipzig).

Das Seelenleben des Jugendlichen, Dr. Charlotte Bühler (Fisher: Jena).

Schule und Charakter, Dr. F. W. Foerster (Schulthess: Zürich).

The Opposite Sexes, Dr. Heilbronn.

Poems and Essays, W. C. Roscoe (ed. R. H. Hutton).

Woman in Europe, Dr. C. G. Jung (article in *The New Adelphi*, September 1928).

. . . . .

Social Psychology, Dr. W. McDougall.

National Welfare and National Decay, Dr. W. McDougall.

Marriage, Count Hermann Keyserling.

Europe, Count Hermann Keyserling (section *France*).

The Evolution of Modern Marriage, F. Müller-Lyer. Translated by I. C. Wigglesworth. (*In preparation*.)

Marriage and the Sex Problem, Dr. F. W. Foerster (Wells Gardner).

The Night-Hoers, A. M. Ludovici.

Population and Birth Control (ed. E. and C. Paul).

Publications of the Eugenics Society (including *The Eugenics Review*).

Archiv für Rassen und Gesellschaftsbiologie.

Race Hygiene and Heredity, Dr. H. W. Siemens.

The Family and the Nation, W. C. D. Whetham and Catherine Whetham.

The Mothers, R. Briffault.

Also the writers referred to on pp. 229–30.

. . . . .

Creative Evolution, Bergson.

Holism and Evolution, J. C. Smuts.

Social Evolution, Benjamin Kidd.

Organische Kultur, R. von Engelhardt.

. . . . .

Time and Tide (weekly periodical).

. . . . .

The works of Jane Austen, George Eliot, George Meredith, Galsworthy, Edith Wharton, H. G. Wells, W. B. Maxwell, D. H. Lawrence.

INDEX

For Product Safety Concerns and Information please contact our EU
representative GPSR@taylorandfrancis.com
Taylor & Francis Verlag GmbH, Kaufingerstraße 24, 80331 München, Germany